ONCE UPON A RHYME

IMAGINATION FOR A NEW GENERATION

London
Edited by Steph Park-Pirie

First published in Great Britain in 2004 by:
Young Writers
Remus House
Coltsfoot Drive
Peterborough
PE2 9JX
Telephone: 01733 890066
Website: www.youngwriters.co.uk

All Rights Reserved

© *Copyright Contributors 2004*

SB ISBN 1 84460 521 3

Foreword

Young Writers was established in 1991 and has been passionately devoted to the promotion of reading and writing in children and young adults ever since. The quest continues today. Young Writers remains as committed to engendering the fostering of burgeoning poetic and literary talent as ever.

This year's Young Writers competition has proven as vibrant and dynamic as ever and we are delighted to present a showcase of the best poetry from across the UK. Each poem has been carefully selected from a wealth of *Once Upon A Rhyme* entries before ultimately being published in this, our twelfth primary school poetry series.

Once again, we have been supremely impressed by the overall high quality of the entries we have received. The imagination, energy and creativity which has gone into each young writer's entry made choosing the best poems a challenging and often difficult but ultimately hugely rewarding task - the general high standard of the work submitted amply vindicating this opportunity to bring their poetry to a larger appreciative audience.

We sincerely hope you are pleased with our final selection and that you will enjoy *Once Upon A Rhyme London* for many years to come.

Contents

Siân Macarty Cole (11)	1
Salome Senhouse (12)	2

Abercorn School

Rebecca Anthony (8)	2
Giorgia Ascolani (9)	3
Sebastian Hallum Clarke (6)	3
Sam Davenport (9)	3
Sam Morris (9)	4
Georgia Summers (10)	5
Carlota Cobiella (9)	6
Louisa Guldberg (9)	6
James Pike-Watson (9)	7
Daniel Vukelich (10)	7
Colleen Nevison (9)	7
Phoebe Norton (10)	8
Danna Elmasry (9)	8
Madeline Bell (8)	9
Hilary Fitzsimmons (10)	9
Angus Smith (9)	10
Zoë Nicola Silkstone (8)	10
Natalia Green (9)	11
Colin Laurence (9)	11
Shikha Pahari (10)	12
Galia Al-Babtain (10)	12
Shaska Charlton Bain (9)	13
Jonathan Velasco (10)	13
Annina Francis (11)	13
Berlinda Middleton (10)	14
Alice Haguenauer (10)	14
Emma Hulme (10)	15
John Hahn (7)	15
Max Ascolani (7)	15
Maya Perkins (7)	15
Jake Schuman-Jackson (7)	16
Natalie Klingher (7)	16
Savannah Henry (7)	16
Madeleine Gledhill (7)	17
Aiko Miyamoto (7)	17

Aleksandar Popovic (7)	17
Nicholas Groll (8)	18
Max Silvestrin (8)	18
Eleanor Thwaites (7)	19
Dylan Van Lengen (7)	19
Francesca Da Costa (7)	20
Harry Pourdjis (7)	20
Raphael Hagenauer (7)	21
John Oswald (11)	21
Jessica Davenport (7)	22
Holly Nevison (7)	22
Kelsey Brown (8)	23
Anirudh Chouhan (7)	23
Melissa Francis (10)	24
William Floyd (9)	24
Kiran D Sharma (9)	25

Canonbury Primary School
Naomi Stock (10)	26

Devonshire House School
Yukitaka Kojima (10)	27
Savvas Procopiou (9)	27
Emilie Heddle (9)	28
Alysia Fox (9)	28
Amaliah Phillips (9)	29
Delara Shakib (10)	29
Dania Arafeh (9)	30
Sophie Pearce (9)	30
Rae Okpu (9)	31
Isabella Martino (9)	32
Orlando Beecroft (8)	32
Maxim Rozhdov (10)	33
Freddie McTavish (10)	33
Madeleine Hardt (10)	34
Sasha Banks (9)	34
Jack Ferera (9)	35
Zeynep Uresin (10)	35
Karishma Choraria (9)	36
Daniella Goodwin (9)	36
David Woon (11)	37

Alexander Woodford (9)	37
Paz Garcia (8)	38
Arike Emanuel (8)	38
Shahzaad Natt (10)	39
David Wong (10)	39
Shyamala Ramakrishna (8)	40

Hartley Primary School

Sounia Ibrahim (10)	41
Sayeeda Ahmed (10)	41
Safiya Butt (9)	41
Thanushan Sriskantharasa (8)	42
Sanjay Nandha (9)	42
Simone Osei-Owusu (11)	42
Sadiya Mahfuza (8)	43
Behina Shah (8)	43
Anisha Ahmed (9)	44
Amina Naseem (9)	44
Shanice Kumarsen (10)	45
Abdul Farooq (8)	45
Nishani Jeyapalan (10)	46
Tehreem Sehar (8)	46
Tahir Khan (10)	47
Janani Jeyanthan & Dorcas Matomby (10)	47
Pirisan Sriskantharasa (11)	48
Nadafia Kauser (9)	48
Jeba Ganapathy (11) & Maariyah Nakhuda (10)	49
Waqas Hussain (9)	49
Hena Zubair (10)	50
Nerogitha Veerasingam (7)	50
Sruti Varsani (9)	51
Avisa Rhaman (10)	51
Ankita Patel (9)	52
Nimisha Makwana (10)	52
Peju Famojuro (11)	53
Krisha Hirani (10)	53
Atiyyah Jabeen Afzal (10)	54
Tarnum Pathan (11)	54
Inesh Porbudas (10)	55
Henna Ayaz (11)	56
Shahida Soomro (11)	57

Rabia Mirza (10) — 58
Jasmin Sehmbi (10) — 59

Orchard Primary School
Jules Mattsson (9) — 59
Yusuf Mohammed (9) — 60
Zainab Hirsi (10) — 60
Tuncay Cager (10) — 60
Julien Winkel Junior (10) — 61
Jithin Selvamon Selvaraj (9) — 61
Jasmine Adekunle (9) — 61
Berkeley Ayemere (10) — 62
Romario (9) — 62
Yeter Altun (10) — 63
Asma Barits (9) — 63
Shannon Palmer-Mutlu (8) — 63
Sophie Allen (8) — 64
Abubakar Siddique (10) — 64
Hanane Taibi (10) — 65
Kwaku Amoah Adamah (9) — 65
Elizabeth Akinyemi (10) — 65
Kaydene Royes (10) — 66
Richard Bryan (10) — 66
Sevcan Cigerit (10) — 66
Farhana Kazi (9) — 67
Sevily Kalen (10) — 67
Miguel Rels Da Silva (9) — 67
Ferdos Daqiq (8) — 68
Foyez Uddin (10) — 68
Tiwalade Oladipupo (8) — 69
Corey Fagan (10) — 69
Lucas Lampetis (8) — 70
Temi Jekennu (8) — 70
Bertan Jafer (8) — 71
Ilham Abdi (8) — 71
Muberra Keven (9) — 72
Esther Fagbola (8) — 72
Rima Begum (7) — 72
Caleb Guthrie (8) — 73
Jessica Le (8) — 73
Jamila Akter Alam (8) — 74

Nazeerah Mangera (8)	75
Nurcan Altun (7)	76
Elisabeth Ekundayo (8)	77
Savvina Ploutarchou (8)	78
Sydni Akiz (8)	79
Demi Daniel (7)	79
Shanara Phillips (8)	80
Ozan Kaya (9)	80
Milton Johnson (9)	81
Shara Oluwole (8)	81
Sarah Parker (9)	82
Alekzander Crook (8)	82
Devinya Thomas (8)	83
Rafi High (8)	83
Vanessa Idehen (7)	84
Yousuf Mahamed (8)	84
Fatima Jagne (7)	85
Patricia Kyei Acheampony (7)	85
Dervon Anthony (9)	86
Jordan Eadon (7)	86
Sabrine Abdou (9)	87
Yusuf Abas Qulaten (10)	88
Nowshin Begum (7)	89
Peri Mustafa (7)	89
Fatha Rahman (9)	90
Ramazan Calli (7)	90
Mosthood Olastan (10)	91
Shernice Best (9)	91
Chevantae Brown (9)	92
Ishtiaq Ahad (10)	93
Daniel Hague (9)	94
Ebony Samuel (9)	95
Haboon Hussein Farid (9)	96
Claire Troung (9)	97
Jade Luong (10)	98
Kemal Kayran (10)	99
Fatima Qulaten (9)	100
Hasan Ali (9)	100
Malik Adeleke (10)	101
Christopher Laye (9)	102
Victoria Ghann (10)	103
Serife Ozicer (10)	104

Burak Pirbudah (10)	105
Naa Oblikai Laryea (9)	106
Dillan Al Bayati (8)	106
Tyler Powell (9)	107
Shamol Miah (9)	108
Jahed Uddin (9)	109
Monisha Alam (9)	110
Stephanie Wong (8)	111
Zaki Muhammed Chowdhury (8)	112
Qasim Hussain (10)	113

St Andrew's JMI School, Totteridge Village

Vishali Patel (7)	113
Georgina Molloy (7)	113
Mayu Noda (7)	114
Amani Momoniat (7)	114
Christian Tye (7)	114
Marcus Burns (7)	114
Lily Kinsley (8)	115
Sean O'Callaghan (7)	115
Cameron Daee (8)	115
Sydney Grace Weare (7)	115

St John's Primary School, Whetstone

Jessica Vize (10)	116
Kelly Warner (11)	116
Hamish Nash (9)	116
Andreas Victoros (9)	117
Jenny Watts (10)	117
Samuel Tan (11)	118
Luke Vincent-Kynaston (10)	118
Ella Berger Sparey (9)	119
Fiona Donaldson (10)	119
Amber Gharebaghi (10)	120
Despina Kefala (11)	120
Hafsah Rashid (9)	121
Eleanor Lovick-Norley (10)	121
Marc Erbil (10)	122
Rosie Stephens (11)	122
James Thicknes (10)	123
Hayley Brooks	123

Laura Moulton (8)	124
Olivia Brown (11)	124
Maisie Bovingdon (11)	125
Kate Hampshire (10)	125
Aastha Bhatt (9)	126
Jamie Byrne (9)	126
Shiraz Kootar (10)	127
Amy Waters (9)	127
Catherine Wright (9)	128
Stephanie Hunter (8)	128
David Luckhurst (10)	129
Aron Boughton (8)	129
Michelle Kyriacou (9)	130
Antonia Pagonis (11)	130
Rhys Hunt (10)	131
Christine Edwards (11)	131
Steven Morris (9)	132
Evangelina Moisi (9)	132
Ming Moore (9)	133
Natasha Solonos (9)	133
Bobbie Burkin (9)	134
Laura Martin (8)	134
Ernestine Hui (10)	135
Pernia Price (9)	135
Ilana Yacobi (9)	136
Thomas Magnitis (8)	136
Meera Patel (11)	136
Jade Kong (9)	137
Anthony Stamatiou (8)	137
Jessica Tarling (9)	138
Cameron Wolfe (9)	138
Luke Erbil (8)	139

Simon Marks' Primary School

Leilah Isaac (11)	139
Beth Oppenheim (10)	140
Dean Joseph	140
Sarah Brown (8)	141
Ella Davies Oliveck (7)	141
Chantelle Arovo (9)	141
Shulamit Morris-Evans (8)	142

Snaresbrook Primary School
Jodie Marriott-Baker (10) — 142
Pippa Wiskin (9) — 143
Daniel Morgan-Thomas (10) — 143
Sehar Ishaq Khan (10) — 144
Lewis Munro (9) — 144
Sanjida Mahmood (10) — 145
Sapphire Sherbird (10) — 145

Stockwell Primary School
Patricia Ogunmodede (11) — 146
Jezzell Ethan Domas (11) — 146
Emranur Rahman (10) — 147
Patricia Asante (7) — 147
Leilah Clarke (10) — 148
Gabriela Costa (8) — 148
Aaron Ford (10) — 149
Cherrelle Rule (10) — 149
Corrine Burrell Matthews (10) — 150
Nandipa Mukosi (7) — 150
Adesola Soyombo (9) — 151
Jeremie Kasonga (10) — 151
Zhané Fritz (8) — 152
Timi Soyombo (7) — 152
Jhannelle (9) — 152
Ellis Thomas (8) — 153
Trey Foster Gonzales (9) — 153
Jennelle Reece-Gardner (9) — 154
Shallise Chaney (8) — 154
Fabiana Martins (10) — 155
Aminah Turay (7) — 155
Donica Bryan (10) — 156
George Foli-Archer (11) — 156
Martina Kissi (10) — 157
Fatima Islam (11) — 157
Marta Santos Faria (11) — 158

Whittingham Community Primary School
Charlotte Louise Corben (10) — 158

The Poems

A Bird In The Snow

I am a bird
A bird with frozen wings,
As the snow lies on the ground
My mother calls and sings.

As she sings upon this morning,
The sun begins to rise
And all the little boys and girls
Start to open their eyes.

The shadow cast against the snow
Sparkles in the sun,
I'll jump out of my nest
And do my best to have a lot of fun.

But as quickly as the snow has come
It sadly begins to melt
And now I realise it is going
I'm expressing how I felt.

I like the snow
I like it lots although it makes me cold,
I hope it snows one time, again
Before I get quite old!

Siân Macarty Cole (11)

Mum's The Word

She makes me laugh
Even when I am down,
She leads me on the right path
To bring me round.

The food from Jamaica is what she loves,
It tastes like Heaven above,
Sent by God's dove.
It's her who I love.
When I was a baby.
She gave me my lovely name
Without her -
Nothing will be the same.

Salome Senhouse (12)

The Dismal Day

As I think and think and think
I see two firemen posing up the street.
Glittering lamp lights glowing
As I look and I hear the neighbours mowing,
I see two sweet robins, fluttering
Past my door.
The sweet peacefulness is ruined
As I hear Mum banging on the upstairs floor!

My cat is purring deep breaths
The robins are fluttering into their nests.
I reach to grab my vest but cold air
Hits me in the chest.
I put my socks on -
My cat catches a fly
I stride out of the room with a big, big sigh.

Rebecca Anthony (8)
Abercorn School

Spiders

I like spiders
Furry and friendly
Likeable legs
Sweet as flowers
Delicate and dangly
Gorgeous googly eyes
As big as a cake
Lovely hairy legs
A big grin.

Giorgia Ascolani (9)
Abercorn School

At The Seaside

Feel the starfish on the rocks,
Taste the ice cream from the ice cream truck.
Smell the salty sea air,
Listen to the splashing waves.
See the crabs crawling in and out of their holes.

Sebastian Hallum Clarke (6)
Abercorn School

The Sun

Sun heat
Covers the land
Forever escaping
From horrible cold windy days
It stays.

Sam Davenport (9)
Abercorn School

Out Of My Window

On Monday, in the afternoon
I come back home from school
Walk a bit along
And dive into a pool!

On Tuesday, in the morning
The milkman comes, hooray!
He gives you milk and orange juice,
I hope he comes today.

On Wednesday, in the afternoon
I come back for dinner,
It's always yummy
Because I'm the winner.

On Thursday, at night-time
When we go to sleep
There is a 'honk' outside
Beep! Beep!

On Friday, in the morning
I eat breakfast soon.
When I get to breakfast time
I'm eating with my spoon.

On Saturday, in the morning
My sister leaves for Germany
I feel so happy
I feel like I'm in harmony.

On Sunday, in the afternoon
I feel so unhappy,
My brothers are downstairs
All wearing nappies!

Sam Morris (9)
Abercorn School

Life Is A Sponge

Oh what's it like to be a sponge
When cleaning hard food and scrubbin' old gunge?'
Oh tell me my brain, as big as a muppet,
Will it be fun? Will I sleep in a closet?'

Dear Sissy, I tell you it's not at all great,
You'll be really scared, you'll have no mate.
It's terrible, horrible, just really bad,
You'll be all alone and sad.

I would know, I once was a sponge
I had to clean food and gunge.
My bro turned me into one with a magic chickpea
It weren't funny but he laughed at me.

I was alone with no one there,
Apart from a teacup and some old hair.

I don't care I wanna be a sponge, a sponge,
I wanna scrub food and gunge.
I don't think it's terrible or bad,
I wanna be alone, I wanna be sad.
You see, being a sponge is my passion,
I don't want the latest fashion . . .
I wanna be a sponge!'

Georgia Summers (10)
Abercorn School

Friends Like You To . . .

Friends like you to . . .
be kind
keep secrets
and be their partner,
when it's school time.

Friends like you to . . .
send them postcards,
take photographs,
and enjoy the ride,
when it's holiday time.

Friends like you to . . .
play with them
eat with them
and talk with them,
when it's home time.

Friends like you to . . .
be quiet
turn off the light
and close your eyes,
when it's bed time.

Carlota Cobiella (9)
Abercorn School

Sea

The sea is calm tonight
Seagulls fly overhead
Curious crabs crawl
On rocky stones.
The waves splash
Against the cliff, so high
Like a gun, shooting at the sky.
The dolphins jump, turn and spin
On and on, they want to swim.

Louisa Guldberg (9)
Abercorn School

Spiders

Spiders
I hate spiders
Big and hairy
Creepy and crawly
Eyes like rubies
Mushy and mashy
Black as cloaks
Scary as nightmares
Fat and frightening
Teeth like taunts.

James Pike-Watson (9)
Abercorn School

Charlie Churchil

Charlie Churchil's cool cat
Caught a coughing cold.
Crazy! thought Charlie,
My cool cat could never catch a cold.
His cat went to the hospital 'cause
Charlie Churchil thought that his cat
Couldn't catch a crazy, coughing cold.

Daniel Vukelich (10)
Abercorn School

The Beach

The sea is calm tonight
The moon is very bright.
People running round and round
A fire on the ground
As big as a brown bear.

Colleen Nevison (9)
Abercorn School

There's A Bee Up My Ear

In the park, a little bee
Came up to my ear and said, 'Tee-hee-hee!'
He flew up my ear in one big whoosh!
Out of my ear
I saw his small fuzzy tush.

'Mum! Mum! There's a bee in my ear!'
'Darling don't tell fibs!'
Mr Bee said, 'Tee-hee-hee!'

The very next day I went to school
And negotiated with the goths -
I heard 'Tee-hee-hee!'
'Try this mate, It's sure to get it out!
Hair spray la goth!'
'You're mad!'

Sprits, sprits, sprits! This isn't working!
Ah-ah the bee is tickling me - tee-hee-hee!
Pop!
The bee is free! Tee-hee-hee!
The very next day the bee came to say -
'Thank you little boy.'
'My pleasure!'

Phoebe Norton (10)
Abercorn School

Lonely And Invisible

I wandered as lonely as a cloud,
Invisible to everyone.
Moving across the sky
As quiet as a mouse.
Swooshing across
The endless blue, as quiet as birds.
Unaware of the things around me.

Danna Elmasry (9)
Abercorn School

My Secret

My friend come close,
I have a secret I want to share.
Yes, that secret is hidden
In my head,
Oh yes, I will share
That secret that I dare
To share, and my secret
That I dare to share is . . .
'Oh there's the bell for lunch.'

Oh my friend, now I promise
I will tell my secret that I dare to share
Because I trust my secret that I dare
To share is safe inside you.
Now listen close my dear, dear friend,
My secret that I dare to share is -
'You're my very best friend.'

Madeline Bell (8)
Abercorn School

Tiger

(Based on 'The Tiger' by William Blake)

Tiger! Tiger! Burning bright
Wandering, watching through the night.
If he catches you, please beware
If he does he'll give you a scare!

Luckily, luckily, you didn't get caught
Because if you did, you'll be a big nought.
Be careful or he'll give you a fright,
And he'll gobble you up, all through the night!

Hilary Fitzsimmons (10)
Abercorn School

Homework

I'm drowning in a sea of homework
So here I go
Scribble, scribble, scribble!

I'm buried in text books from head to toe,
Scribble, scribble!

My pencil is broken,
I'm raring to stop but my teacher has spoken,
So I will work till the job is done!

At last, I'm done -
But a terrible thought returns to my head
Because of the memory of what my teacher said:
'If you don't study for the test, you'll be doing
Tonnes of homework without a second's rest!'

Angus Smith (9)
Abercorn School

Out Of My Window

I look out of my window and what can I hear and see?
I can see and hear people walking and squelching
through the slushy snow.
I can also see bare grey, wintry trees.
The seagulls are squawking and the blustery winds
are swirling through the pouring snow.
The tall buildings lost in the low clouds and the sound of cars
whizzing past one another.
The traffic lights are turning red, orange and green every few seconds!
Wow! I never knew there were so many things outside my window!

Zoë Nicola Silkstone (8)
Abercorn School

Tiger
(Based on 'The Tiger' by William Blake)

Tiger! Tiger! Burning bright
His fur is orange, shining light.
Black stripes across this scary mammal,
Smooth and sleek, not like the camel!
Shining, sliding, slithering, like a snake,
Everywhere is food to make.
Run, run to the annexe!
Everyone run. Oh no! Mr Mannexe!
Get a doctor! Oh great!
Gulp!
The tiger has eaten Mr Mannexe with a
Gulp!

Natalia Green (9)
Abercorn School

The Red-Eyed Blue Bug Eater

The red-eyed blue bug eater is a very strange bird,
Its general appearance is absolutely absurd.
It has a long neck with two red eyes,
When it's in the mood, it flaps its legs and flies.

It is hard to spot because it lives in a hole,
It has a large range which is south of the South Pole.
Its usual cry is, 'Coo-coo! Coo-coo!
The only time you will see one is in the zoo.

Colin Laurence (9)
Abercorn School

The Beach

Glistening waves dance in the sea
Crashing against the towering cliffs,
A dense shroud of mist trapping me
Bars of purple clouds glide through the air.

The flaming sun sets behind the vast blue ocean,
The sullen heavy clouds appear,
This is a romantic location over here.
It fills my cup of joy with emotion.

White foam gurgles,
As grey floods water,
The rough sea slaughters the shells in half,
As a stiff wind blew.

The stunning shells in extraordinary shapes,
Perched on the velvety sand.
Slimy masses of seaweed thrash against the land.

The seagulls reach their destination,
As they soar towards the snowy mountains,
And they chant their magical incantation,
With their atmospheric 'quack!'

Green waves curled and arched as they shimmer in the moonlight,
The vague reflection scribbled on the ocean
As I sit and apply lotion.

Shikha Pahari (10)
Abercorn School

Tiger! Tiger!

(Based on 'The Tiger' by William Blake)

Tiger! Tiger! Burning bright,
Can you see the shining light.
The tiger's teeth were as sharp as a knife
Hoping you won't lose your life.
I was as afraid as a mouse,
Which creeps around the house.

Galia Al-Babtain (10)
Abercorn School

The Evening Beach

The sea is calm tonight,
the clouds all loom up in the sky.
The seaweed sways gently
in the foamy waves.
The sand slides back and forth
rolling into a surface
as soft as pastry.

Shaska Charlton Bain (9)
Abercorn School

Cats And Dogs

Cat
scratchy, fury
licking, scratching, fighting,
nice, peaceful, slob, disgusting
sneezing, slobbering, fighting
friendly, joyful
Dog.

Jonathan Velasco (10)
Abercorn School

Teacher - Student

Teacher
strict   nice
teaching, working, smirking
shouts, screams, small, tiny
learning, reading, writing
weak   smart.
Student.

Annina Francis (11)
Abercorn School

Snake

Snakes
Slither and slide
Through the leaves, on
The Amazon floor.
Their skin colour makes them
Camouflaged on the floor.
They swallow you whole,
As if they wanted you to have
A painful death.

Their fangs are
Shining, like daggers.
Glistening in the sun,
They are ready to strike
On you and on other prey!

Berlinda Middleton (10)
Abercorn School

The First Day Of School

A million billion people staring and glaring at me,
When I walk into the Assembly Room.
What's the time, am I late?
Have I wet my pants, are my trousers down?
Mr Badminton is looking at me, what should I do?
Will he throw a badminton shuttlecock at me?
It's in his hand. Aaargh, help me!

Alice Haguenauer (10)
Abercorn School

Teachers

Tall loud
shouting, walking, talking
cross, angry, empty, soft
sitting, listening, playing
short quiet
Students.

Emma Hulme (10)
Abercorn School

Transport Just Goes Everywhere!

Transport just goes everywhere
Wherever you want it to go.
So jump on board a plane, train or ship
And ask where you want to go!

John Hahn (7)
Abercorn School

Football

Kick the ball
Use your head,
Dribble the ball
And then you score!

Max Ascolani (7)
Abercorn School

Whiskey Inside The Ball

Whiskey went in the ball,
He rolled and bumped his head.
Then he wiggled around the chair
And he bumped his head again!

Maya Perkins (7)
Abercorn School

Tiger
(Based on 'The Tiger' by William Blake)

I am a tiger,
If you come near me,
I might *growl!*
If you come closer
I might *bite!*
My favourite food is human beings . . .
So watch out!

Jake Schuman-Jackson (7)
Abercorn School

Brothers

Big and smelly.
Mean and nasty.
They punch me a lot.
They tease me too much.
I have two of them.
That means twice as much pain.
Sometimes I wish I could just
Lock them up.

Natalie Klingher (7)
Abercorn School

Snow

Snow!
Snow is white and soft,
It is fun to play with.
I *love it!*

Savannah Henry (7)
Abercorn School

Colours

Purple is a lovely flower blooming in the spring,
Blue is a waxy crayon that melts under fire.
Red is a round ball bouncing when you throw it,
Green is a rough tree bending as it blows in the wind.
Yellow is a pretty sun shining in the sky.

Madeleine Gledhill (7)
Abercorn School

Colours

Pink is a dusty pig rolling in the mud
Red is a round shiny apple ready to eat
Orange is a hard book waiting to be opened
Green is a fluffy slipper under the bed.

Aiko Miyamoto (7)
Abercorn School

When It's Snowing . . .

When it's snowing I get to make a snowman,
When it's snowing I get to make a snowball,
When it's snowing, it's fun to get wet,
When it's snowing you get all snowy!

Aleksandar Popovic (7)
Abercorn School

Out Of My Window

Today I can see . . .
Dogs barking in the pound,
Snow falling on the ground.
Cars crashing
Pigeons smashing
Children dressing up as knights
And people having a snowball fight.
Cars crashing
Pigeons smashing.

Today I can smell . . .
The leather of my shoes
Dog poo on you
Cars crashing
Pigeons smashing.

Today I can hear . . .
The galloping of a horse
The wind, of course.

Cars crashing, pigeons smashing,
Cars crashing, pigeons smashing.
What's next?

Nicholas Groll (8)
Abercorn School

My Sister

I have a sister called Maya
She is always a liar
She sits on a fire and she's always a crier
And that's why she's called Maya.

Max Silvestrin (8)
Abercorn School

Five Senses

I like the taste of marmalade
Tickling on my tongue

I like the feel of my toes
Tiptoeing in my ballet shoes

I like the sound of robins
Tweeting in my ears

I like the feel of my puppy
Cuddling around my feet

I like the look of my sister
Talking in my face

I like the smell of roses
Tingling up my nose.

Eleanor Thwaites (7)
Abercorn School

Five Senses

I like the look of my kitten
Running around my house.

I like the smell of sweets
Melting as they touch my tongue.

I like the sound of a snake
Hissing around my neck.

I like the look of Lego fighters
Doing cool stuff.

I like the taste of a Twix
Crunching in my mouth.

Dylan Van Lengen (7)
Abercorn School

Colours

Blue is a lovely sky
making everything bright

Purple is a very soft jumper
itching me

Yellow is a beautiful sunflower
growing each day

Orange is a waxy crayon
which melts under fire

Pink is a soft cushion
waiting for you to sit on it.

Green is a colourful pen
writing on the board.

Francesca Da Costa (7)
Abercorn School

Five Senses

I like the feel of the soap in my daddy's bath
slipping in my hands

I like the sound of balloons
popping in my ears

I like the smell of roses
tickling my nose

I like the taste of chicken
burning in the oven

I like the look of the sea
waving in the ocean.

Harry Pourdjis (7)
Abercorn School

The Strange Dog

There was a dog
Who ate a log
He kept on talking
But he couldn't stand the walking
He sat on the cat
And squashed it flat

He was a very strange dog
He could see in the fog
He drove a car
He drank in a bar
All he had for friends
Were hens and
He went swimming in the River Thames

He had a hat
And called it Pat
He had a cat
And called it Tat.

Raphael Hagenauer (7)
Abercorn School

A Ranger

A ranger is light green
He is summertime in the park.
He is bright,
A ranger wears a green uniform,
A tall grandfather clock.
He is an animal show and
A roast hamburger!

John Oswald (11)
Abercorn School

Poland

In Poland there was lots of snow
Frostbite came up to my big toe,
I loved my friends there,
Those kinds of friends are very rare.
But my friends here are just as good
They all eat my delicious pud.
I love the school here as well,
Except in break time, when I hear the bell.
In Poland, when it was cold
My dad made biscuits which I sold.
This year I'm going to Cairo
And buy a golden biro.
In Cairo it is warm
There's not a single storm,
I miss Poland so much,
Though Poland and I are still in touch.

Jessica Davenport (7)
Abercorn School

Canada

When I go back to Canada I hope there
Will be snow, and I want it to grow
And grow and grow.
When I go on the hills I can slide and
I can ski, just before tea.
When I make a snowman I think
I will make two,
I'll name them Moo and Hoo.
When I'm done, I'll have some hot chocolate
That's just what I'll do!

Holly Nevison (7)
Abercorn School

My Biggest Secret

I think I'm ready to tell my secret
But I really don't know.
The secret I know is really good
I might just not tell.
Don't get mad,
I know I might
If my friend won't tell me hers,
It's a very great secret.

No, I won't give away my secret
Even though I said I would
I guess I wasn't ready
Did you really think I could?
My secret is really important
Do not believe my lie
For if I tell my secret
My heart will surely die.

Kelsey Brown (8)
Abercorn School

Tanks

I am green like the grass,
I shoot big, black missiles.
I carry army people,
I am very *big* and heavy.

Anirudh Chouhan (7)
Abercorn School

Out Of My Window

Out of my window
Where I look every day,
I see a hopping squirrel
They get cuter as I talk my way.

Out of my window,
Where I see some flapping birds,
They start to sing
As I had never heard.

Out of my window
Where I see a tall green tree.
I like the way I am
As small as I can be.

Melissa Francis (10)
Abercorn School

Something To Tell You

There is something I want to tell you
that I haven't told you yet,
but don't tell anyone
not until you're let.
I've been hiding it for quite a while now and
don't get too excited
or have a cow.
I hope I've made you happy now
that I have told you
So I'll tell you something else because I've
nothing better to do.

William Floyd (9)
Abercorn School

Out Of My Window

Out of my window I can see
An overgrown forest with big tall trees.
Out of my window rabbits are running
For good reason, a fox is coming.

In the forest, a watery sky,
Some beautiful flowers going by.
My neck is hurting from looking out,
I think I should stroll back into the house.
But alas, the scene is so beautiful.

I run downstairs,
I take two pairs.
I run to the road
Following a mole.
I run to the border
I go no further
Until I see
A fox pouncing.

I jump in the way
And there I lay
For the rest of the day
And there I seem to stay.
The next day I wake up
I stand up right
I get quite a fright.
When I look at my watch,
It has stopped!

I run back to the house,
I see a mouse,
I shut my eyes
I see black skies.

Kiran D Sharma (9)
Abercorn School

My Street

Round the corner into my street
Stare through the window of house number one
The Romans lounge on sofas neat.

Glance through the window of house number three
Water floods the floor
The mermaids flick their scaly tails,
As if they're in the sea.

Gaze at house number five
The curtains are drawn, the lights are off
I wonder if they're alive?

At number seven, an old lady looks out
Her cats cling to the ceiling and chairs,
Tails curl and swish, there's one cat called Scout.

There's crying at number nine
A new baby boy is as red as a raspberry
The floor has teddies set up in a line.

I glimpse into number eleven
The super-techno computer wiz
Doesn't look up, he's only seven!

Thirteen is the musical one
Blasting the trumpet, tooting the flute
Everyone makes music right to the youngest son.

By the time I'm at house fifteen
My bag is heavy, I trudge on by
Shrubs, lavender, daffodils and roses
Beginning to lean.

Seventeen
Next stop - my house
Unlock the green door
Shoes off! Collapse!

Naomi Stock (10)
Canonbury Primary School

Ruud Van Nistelrooy Kenning

Football-kicker,
Goal-scorer,
Best-player,
Master-dribbler,
Penalty-master,
Spot-kick-taker,
Corner-kick-receiver,
Ball-striker,
Shot-curler,
Ball-lifter,
Lob-receiver,
Tap-in-expert,
Hat-trick-scorer,
Top-scorer,
That's why he's the best.

Yukitaka Kojima (10)
Devonshire House School

Tiger

Child-eater
Stripy-killer
Jungle-lover
Animal-hunter
Teeth-barer
Meat-eater
Quiet-walker
Big-mouth
Mouth-drooler
Loud-growler.

That is your warning!

Savvas Procopiou (9)
Devonshire House School

A Perfect Me

Brilliant gymnast
Great hockey player . . . at last
Very lively
I've been all these things recently!
I'm excellent at footy
I can easily turn into a cutie
I'm especially good at netball
And my exam marks never fall
I can win any card game
Every day is just the same
I can solve any trick
I mean everyone thinks I'm thick
I can handle sprouts
I never have any doubts
I think I'm cool
Because all the girls say I rule
Oh, if only that were true.

Emilie Heddle (9)
Devonshire House School

Loads Of Sweets

Loads of treats
Fizzy fish and
Liquorice
Marshmallows,
Fudge brownies,
Hubba Bubba,
Blackcurrant is my favourite
Sweets, loads of sweets
Yummy
Which one is your favourite?

Alysia Fox (9)
Devonshire House School

Sweet Shop

Candy treats,
Sour sweets,
Bubble gum,
In my tum.
Starmix,
Liquorice
Hubba Bubba
And banana
Strawberry,
Raspberry,
Pineapple.
Jelly bubble,
Chocolate in my tum,
I love to say, *'Yum yum, yum!'*
Cherry drops,
Lollipops,
Vines of chewy limes,
Jar of chewy, gooey crocodile chimes.
Apple chunks,
Gooey gunk,
A pile of junk.

Amaliah Phillips (9)
Devonshire House School

A School Playground

The school playground made the most peculiar noises today;
It shrieked when people fell flat on it,
It cackled like a herd of hyenas,
It groaned when people were hungry,
It sloshed when people ran through the muddy snow,
It murmured when people gossiped,
It scudded when the football shot across its surface,
But when the bell rang it fell dead silent.

Delara Shakib (10)
Devonshire House School

The Spell
(Story based on a witch who is going to cook up a child)

This is a spell that will make you shiver
I'll fry their bones and cut their liver
I'll put in a spider, a frog and Daddy's hog,
And a sprinkle of hot red *blood*
And some water from the flood
Then it's time to get the child
I'll make it soggy, wet and mild
I'll squish them, squash them
Put them in my pot
And make some dinner for my hungry lot
Now she's all crispy, crunchy
Ready to eat
You can't even hear her heart beat
Oh, that's lovely, I've eaten her head
Now it's time for another child to be *dead*.

Dania Arafeh (9)
Devonshire House School

Mom's Handbag

Chocolate wrapper
Nit catcher
Yoghurt pot
And, oh my gosh!
A fishing rod
A flying dragon
And a wizard wagon
A pack of tissues
With a lump of sugar
A computer
Oh dear!
A lump of lead.

I hope your mom is more sensible than mine.

Sophie Pearce (9)
Devonshire House School

Mom's Handbag

Red lipstick, 100 pounds,
A gold ring that she lost and found.
A tube of gel,
And a card for Nell.
A plastic snake,
And a homemade cake.
A bottle of Coke,
And a witch's cloak.
My dad's ties,
And a list of pies.
A tube of mascara,
And the keys of the car.
And a palm,
And a clock with an alarm.
A CD player,
And a book called *Layers*.
A nice phone,
With a good tone.
A lump of beef,
And some golden teeth.
A picture of Dad,
And the cat that was bad.
A bottle of wine,
And a book about vines.
Do you think *your* mom will have all these things?

Rae Okpu (9)
Devonshire House School

Sweet Shop

Lollipops
And cherry drops
Pineapple cops,
Mango knops.

Cocktails,
And liquorice snails,
Ice creams,
And chocolate beans.

Wham bars,
And sticky tar,
Bubblegum,
In my tum.
TNT and a bottle of coke,
Those were the last words that I spoke.

Isabella Martino (9)
Devonshire House School

In The Attic

In the attic there is . . .
A thing that goes bump in the night, help!
A moaning ghost, uh-oh!
A poltergeist, argh!
A spider, eeek!
A rat, eeuuww!
A zombie, oh no!
The ghost of Sir Walter Raleigh, argh!
And my sister, *oh Lord help me!*
Oh yeah, she's screaming her head off.

Orlando Beecroft (8)
Devonshire House School

My Bedroom

In my bedroom lay some things that are so weird
Beyond imagination, there are . . .
Scratched computers,
Traps and mazes,
Broken pens and erasers,
Half ripped books,
Fully sharpened hooks,
Hammers, nails and razors,
Tortured cats,
Snapped baseball bats,
Broken glass and rusted brass
Prickly paper, torn blazer,
What's this?
An atomic bomb!
5, 4, 3, 2,1, *booooooom!*

Maxim Rozhdov (10)
Devonshire House School

Sweets

Sweets are like delicious delicacies,
They are as sweet as a sugar cane stick,
They look as yummy as a giant pie,
And I love them like my mum.

Sweets are little white angels,
They are as sticky as my cat's tongue,
They smell as good as a red rose,
And I eat them like a pig!

Freddie McTavish (10)
Devonshire House School

A Teacher's Desk

A mouldy cake,
A sheet saying: 'A clock to make'.
A mini TV showing the Pink Panther,
My book, with all the wrong answers.
A wilted bunch of flowers,
A note saying: 'Take a shower!'
The answers to last week's test,
A poster saying: 'English is the best!'
A laptop with a broken screen,
A jar with one jellybean.
An open can of pork,
A rusty knife and fork.
Confiscated candy,
A coat belonging to Mandy.
A torn dictionary,
A sign saying: 'Go Mary!'

Madeleine Hardt (10)
Devonshire House School

Things In My Bed!

A Goosebumps book,
A plastic snake,
A slimy glob,
A squashed cake,
A ghoul's game with a grunt,
A wet pencil that was blunt,
A mouldy tart on my ted,
A horrid mess in my bed,
So don't sleep in it!

Sasha Banks (9)
Devonshire House School

Winter

Raindrops pattering on the floor,
The house clinging to its front door,
All the animals hiding from bad weather,
Having to sail is being a bother.
Throwing snowballs at your mate,
Throwing away your old slate.
Snowflakes falling on the ground,
Not making a single sound.
Playing with their fantastic toys,
Some of them make a lot of noise.
Making snowmen in the morn,
Some of them do not finish until dawn.
Snow, snow that is all I have to say
I shall write again some other day.

Jack Ferera (9)
Devonshire House School

The Big Sea

The sea is a large aquarium,
It is a blue demon,
Which is deadly and fierce,
He takes people and rushes them from side to side,
He is a roaring lion who goes from big roar to little roar.
But he calms down when the sun is up; he lets his victims enjoy the sun,
You can't hear him move,
He is as silent as the sun.

Zeynep Uresin (10)
Devonshire House School

Five Pets A Fairy Could Own

Meet Wanda and her pets,
A dog that eats pizza,
A spider that makes a huge mess,
A frog that gave her a headache,
He sang all day what could she say?
A cat that slept all day;
She really didn't know what to say.
Nothing compared
To the snake that whistled,
It really got on her nerves,
She really wished she'd
Never won the grand prize!

Karishma Choraria (9)
Devonshire House School

Where The Fairies Go

In the dark of the night, where the fairies go,
Is a little old cottage covered in snow.
They go there because of the nice, warm fire,
And Blossom, the youngest, is a little liar.
Mable, the oldest, takes care of the lot,
And all of the babies are planning a plot.
When dinner is ready everyone runs to the table,
And the older fairies are sometimes disabled.
But most important of all is a little pixie,
Whose name happens to be Trixie.
But their favourite place ever to go,
Is that little old cottage covered in snow.

Daniella Goodwin (9)
Devonshire House School

Witches Brew To Die For

In a witch's cauldron there are
Rotten eggs
Tiger's innards
Newt's eye
Chip of skull of Christ
Scum out of the bath
A rotten whale's calf
Baby's finger
Time doesn't linger
Toenails
Dragon's scales
Owlet's wing
Nasty thing
Child's scalp and hair
And a fox's bloody ear
Blood of baboon
Rotten watermelon
Plastic bags of vomit, Gromit
Wallace's best friend
All these things I love to boil, including a bit of cod liver oil.

David Woon (11)
Devonshire House School

In A Whale's Belly

A whale has
Ten little ships,
Two pirate ships,
A drunken crew,
A couple of islands,
And about two pubs,
A hundred fish or two,
Two mermaids, dead that is,
Two cities and ten towns
And Africa with a few tribes.

Alexander Woodford (9)
Devonshire House School

My Special Teddy Bear

My special teddy bear,
Likes to sit on my chair,
With her padded paws and nose,
She likes to stand all day and pose.

In front of the camera is her favourite place,
Apart from my bed,
She cuddles up and snuggles up,
And then sleeps on my head!

When we're snuggled up in bed,
She climbs back down and winks,
With her purple mysterious eyes,
Then she'll start to blink.

My teddy's name is Lily,
She's all soft, white and pink,
You'd think she's always dirty,
But that's not what I think!

Paz Garcia (8)
Devonshire House School

Valentine's

Valentine is kind,
As you may find.
It is not rude,
With an attitude.
You may think I mean nice,
But think twice.
It is not behind you,
But inside you.
This is a great, big
Valentine!

Arike Emanuel (8)
Devonshire House School

Computer

Hyper-driver
Laser-machine
Nerd-toy
Freak-gizmo
Hi-tech-deck
Key-board
Geek-play
Controlling-dream
Monitor-lean
Hyper-clean
Modern-thing
Printer-plug
Cyber-tub
Memory-whole
Internet-supplier
Palm pilot-server
Kid-fun
Adult-dumb
Port-hole
USB-modem
CD-burner
Helpful-learner.

Shahzaad Natt (10)
Devonshire House School

Mirror

The sea is reflecting the sky
Because he has no real look,
He copies the colour
Just to be like the sky,
He even copies the clouds
By smashing himself on the rocks,
He also copies the sun
By having the sand by his side.

David Wong (10)
Devonshire House School

The Sneaky Cat

It stalked down the steps of the house,
Quiet as a mouse,
Who was that?
It was the sneaky cat!
It went up to a desk,
And there it made a mess,
Who was that?
It was the sneaky cat.
It crept to the hall,
And unrolled a yarn ball,
Who was that?
It was the sneaky cat.
It walked up to the playroom,
And turned the toy box upside down,
Who was that?
It was the sneaky cat.
It took out a squeaky toy,
And that made a noise.
The kids rushed down,
It was enough to astound,
The messed up desk with papers on the ground,
The long string of yarn,
The upside down toy box,
Who was under that?
No one but *the sneaky cat.*

Shyamala Ramakrishna (8)
Devonshire House School

A E I O U

A E I O U
That is how we say them

A E I O U
That is how we play them
We say them loud
We say them soft
We say them anyway we want

A E I O U
That is how we play them.

Sounia Ibrahim (10)
Hartley Primary School

Happiness

My happiness is as red as a rosebush,
It tastes of sweet and luscious strawberries,
It smells of perfumes, looks like a birthday present,
Sounds like cheerful birds singing,
It is blissful, glad and makes me happy.

Sayeeda Ahmed (10)
Hartley Primary School

Happiness

My happiness is as blue as the ocean,
It tastes of luscious blueberry,
It smells of bluebells and looks like a cosy chair,
It sounds like a friendly whale splashing in the sea,
It's joyful and makes me feel delighted.

Safiya Butt (9)
Hartley Primary School

The Mermaid

A mermaid sat on a sandy rock
And her eyes gleamed soft and green,
'Come with me,' she called,
'And I'll take you away to the land beneath the sea.
We'll ride on a dolphin and eat seaweed cake for our tea.'
She held out her hand as she dived through the waves,
'Come with me,
    Come with me,
        Come with me.'

Thanushan Sriskantharasa (8)
Hartley Primary School

My Happiness

My happiness is as yellow as a great sun.
It tastes as sweet as a juicy mango.
Its fragrance is a juicy, ripe red apple.
When I look at something it always reminds me
of David Beckham's hair style.
It sounds like the huge waves in the sea.
It feels like I'm on top of an icy mountain.

Sanjay Nandha (9)
Hartley Primary School

What Can I See Outside My Window?

I remember it like yesterday
A light breeze
It was amazing
The trees trotted down the hill
The bag flew by with crystals.

Simone Osei-Owusu (11)
Hartley Primary School

Nightfall

Nightfall has come
I am asleep
I am tightly tucked in my bed
I can't go to sleep
I wake up
And open the window
Look out and say
'Nightfall has come, make a wish'
But I remember I can't make a wish without a shooting star
I am desperate to make a wish
Then it happened, there was a shooting star
I made the wish
I was so happy
My wish was that
Nightfall would come every year and in the morning as well
I woke up the next morning
It came true
I was so happy
I made a song, it went like this -
Nightfall has come
My wish has come true
I want to cry
But I can't, my wish has come true.

Sadiya Mahfuza (8)
Hartley Primary School

Snow

Snowflakes fell like cotton balls throughout the night
I woke up in the morning and to my delight
The garden was covered like a fluffy blanket of white
Snow was smooth, clean and frosty white.
Catching snowflakes on sugary lakes,
Winter is the king of snowmen.
I am sorry when it is slushy and goes away.

Behina Shah (8)
Hartley Primary School

Love

Love is nothing to hide,
Love is nothing to fight,
If you just read between the lines,
You'll find that it's something special.

Love makes a relationship,
Love makes it work,
From friendship to love,
From all the stars above.

What I see is what I dream,
What I dream is what I see,
But what I dream of is you.

When I look at you it makes me frown,
But thinking of you is a crown,
Friendship is not enough,
But love is oh so tough.

People think that friendship is heaven,
But I can prove them wrong,
His is what matters,
A simple love song.

Anisha Ahmed (9)
Hartley Primary School

Aniworld

The bird said, 'I glide.'
The snake said, 'I slide.'
The mouse said, 'I creep.'
The deer said, 'I leap.'
The dog said, 'I bark.'
The squirrel said, 'I run in the park.'
The cow said, 'I moo.'
Amina said, *'Boo!'*

Amina Naseem (9)
Hartley Primary School

Friendship

Friends are there for you, when you are low
That is why you should never pack your bags and go
Give them a chance to show them how you feel,
Because you never know when your friendship's real.
Your true friends will be there forever,
Keep those promises you made together.
If you had one true friend,
They will be with you right to the end.
Keep your friends close to heart,
Because you never realise you have them till you lose them,
And when you've lost them, you can't get them back . . .
Your friends will be there for you
No matter what you do.
You may not meet, but our words may be few,
But no less sweet is friendship true.
Your true friends will never break up with you for silly reasons,
For if they did, they aren't your true friends.
You true friends will only be your only friends in your heart,
And they will never leave your heart,
Don't break up you will never know how to make up.

*It's OK when three strangers become best friends,
But it's sad when three best friends become strangers . . .*

Shanice Kumarsen (10)
Hartley Primary School

Bad Cat

There was a cat
She was very fat
Her name was Kelly
One day she ate my jelly
She liked to fight
And also bite
She was the worst cat on the planet.

Abdul Farooq (8)
Hartley Primary School

A Road To The Future

Here's me thinking all the way back
About the things that happened
The bombs, the death, the people that cried
Always wondering, wondering why?

Here's me thinking all the way back
About my school and friends
The teachers, the pencils, the work I've done
Was it all just for fun?

Here's me thinking all the way back
When I passed the flight of the air
With an A, an A+ and a B too
I've become a doctor; what I've wanted to do.

Now I'm thinking in the future beyond
With a family, friends and children too
Now that I've achieved what I wanted to do
That is to help in what they're going through!
A road to the future . . .

Nishani Jeyapalan (10)
Hartley Primary School

What Will You Do?

What will you do?
What will you do if you break the table?
What will you do if you rip the bed?
What will you do if you break the fire?
What will you do?
What will you do if you rip the paper?
What will you do if you break the cupboard?
What will you do if you rip the pillow?

I will . . .

Tehreem Sehar (8)
Hartley Primary School

The Magic Fountain

Over the hills, down the mountain,
Step by step I get closer to the fountain,
Up in the air, down on the ground,
The fountain is not to be found.

I took my map, nothing was found,
So I tore it and fell to the ground.
Oh no! The map has been destroyed,
Please God hit me with a raging asteroid.

My wish had come true, what a delight,
As the asteroid rushed next to me, what a sight.
Attached to the asteroid which was on the ground,
The magic fountain, it had been found.

Tahir Khan (10)
Hartley Primary School

Romeo And Juliet Poem

Juliet, Juliet you are the sea which I overflow in with love.
Romeo, Romeo you are the handsome prince that unlocked the door to my heart.
Juliet, Juliet you are like the wind which blows my heart away.
Romeo, Romeo you are the silver shield which protects me from evilness.
Juliet, Juliet your hair is as silky as the everlasting river.
Romeo, Romeo your eyes are the glistening stars.
Juliet, Juliet you are an angel flying upon the heavens.
Romeo, Romeo you are the moon which eclipse over the sun which is I.

Janani Jeyanthan & Dorcas Matomby (10)
Hartley Primary School

Football Story

This is the foot
That kicked the ball.

This is the foot
That kicked the ball
That scored the goal.

This is the foot
That kicked the ball
That scored the goal
That won the cup.

This is the foot
That kicked the ball
That scored the goal
The won the cup
Was played in our yard.

Pirisan Sriskantharasa (11)
Hartley Primary School

Happy Birthday

H stands for hooray,
A stands for adorable,
P stands for party,
P stands for presents,
Y stands for yahoo.

B stands for brilliant,
I stands for invitation,
R stands for roll on,
T stands for temptation,
H stands for hotel,
D stands for determine,
A stands for arrangement,
Y stands for your birthday.

Nadafia Kauser (9)
Hartley Primary School

The Room Of Wonder

I stood in a room full of angels,
And I was led to Heaven above the skies.

I stood in a room full of drummers,
And my heart began to beat loudly.

I stood in a room full of magic,
And my body began to sparkle as brightly as the sun.

I stood in a room full of lies,
And my nose grew longer.

I stood in a room full of sin,
And blackness grew in my heart.

I stood in a room full of rockets,
And got dizzy while I was flying to space.

I stood in a room full of silence,
And felt that death was drawing closer to me.

I stood in a room full of peace,
And saw myself surrounded by doves.

I stood in a room full of mummies,
And wrapped my eyes with fear.

Jeba Ganapathy (11) & Maariyah Nakhuda (10)
Hartley Primary School

Fear

My fear is as red as vampire's blood.
It tastes like raw fish.
It smells like blood and looks like lungs.
It looks like broken legs.
It sounds like a creaking door.
It feels like crunched up pieces of paper.

Waqas Hussain (9)
Hartley Primary School

The Garden Of Spring

As I walk through the garden of spring,
Beneath the golden sun,
The first thing that I hear
Is the songs of the birds.

The cheerful days show me
The nice pale blue sky,
With a touch of pure white,
And the blooming blossoms
Swaying side to side.

In the cool breeze the butterflies fly high above
Fluttering their wings
Beneath the golden fire ball
On a summery day.

As I walk out of the garden of spring
Leaving the birds and the fluttering butterflies,
I enter the days of summer,
Under the burning golden sun.

Hena Zubair (10)
Hartley Primary School

Snow

Snow falls when it is winter.
Snow falls at Christmas.
Snow turns into ice and it will be cold.
Snow is cold.
Snow turns into ice and makes us fall and it's slippery.
When snow falls the sky will be blue.
Snow is white.
When you touch the snow your hands will be cold and freezing.

Nerogitha Veerasingam (7)
Hartley Primary School

My Butterfly

My butterfly is very bright
and when you look at it it's a wonderful sight.
My butterfly can fly up so high
and can also eat your delicious pie.
My butterfly can flap its wings so hard
that it might break through a corrugated card.
My butterfly loves buns
so much but hates the cake crumbs.
My butterfly has lovely eyes
but hates to eat flies.
My butterfly has such long wings
but it never stings.
And finally, my butterfly is so scared of the dark,
so at night between 10 and 11 it never goes to the park.

Sruti Varsani (9)
Hartley Primary School

My Poem About Winter

When I wake up the cold breezes come to me
Like if they want to take me out to the snow.

When it's dark I look up to the sky,
The moon is a white snowball.

In our house we have big a Christmas tree
And where the golden balls twinkle
It looks like the stars are alive.

When it's dark I sit next to the fire
Like there's no heat and have a hot drink.

Avisa Rhaman (10)
Hartley Primary School

Bug Chant

Fighting bugs, biting bugs,
Little nasty writing bugs.

Rain bugs, insane bugs,
Riding on the plane bugs.

Lie bugs, sly bugs,
Find them in your pie bugs.

Shy bugs, cry bugs,
Find them with your eye bugs.

Trick bugs, quick bugs,
Very, very sick bugs.

Free bugs, knee bugs,
Swimming in your tea bugs.

Air bugs, flare bugs,
Find them everywhere bugs.

So just bug off!

Ankita Patel (9)
Hartley Primary School

Coaster

Coaster is lost,
How much did he cost?
I don't want another one.
Make a lost poster,
I'll look for a picture.
Why don't you draw it?
I can never draw Coaster,
Oh I thought we were talking about a toaster.

Nimisha Makwana (10)
Hartley Primary School

The Night Of The Ghost

I went out
to the shops
While I was walking about
I got lost
The trees shook
I kept thinking I must
get back home
The street got darker
I'm all alone
What was that?
Ohh! Ohh! Ohh!
Who is it
behind you?
Where are you
Here!
No you're not
I'm a ghost
Ahhhh!
What . . . what is it?

Peju Famojuro (11)
Hartley Primary School

Dolphin Haiku

Come and swim with me
It will be a joyful time
I can do some tricks.

Krisha Hirani (10)
Hartley Primary School

Never Marry A Horse

Never marry a horse
They're clumsy of course
They don't even have a place to stay
Only on a stack of hay.

They will neigh all over the place
They will gallop around
And everyone will be on the chase.

They won't be at home
You'll find them in the Millennium Dome
They will be on dates with different girls
And buying them necklaces with pearls.

They will be so lazy
That will drive you crazy
Don't marry a horse
You will surely want a divorce.

Atiyyah Jabeen Afzal (10)
Hartley Primary School

I Wandered Lonely As A . . .

I wandered lonely as a leaf
Twisting and turning as I go down
Crunching and crackling as I touch the ground
With the wind blowing me all around.

As I start my journey all ruby and red
With nothing at all I am no longer fed
Without the sun shining and the sky all grey
I have no time to stop and lay.

Tarnum Pathan (11)
Hartley Primary School

The Snowman

Mother, while you were at the shops,
And I was snoozing in my chair,
I heard a tap at the window,
Saw a snowman standing there.

He looked so cold and miserable,
I almost could have cried,
So I put the kettle on,
And invited him inside.

I made him a cup of cocoa,
To warm the cockles of his nose,
Then he snuggled in front of the fire,
For a cosy little doze.

He lay there warm and smiling,
Softly counting sheep,
I eavesdropped for a little while,
Then I too fell asleep.

Seems he awoke and tiptoed out,
Exactly when I'm not too sure,
It's a wonder you didn't see him,
As you came in through the door.

(Oh, and by the way,
The kitten's made a puddle on the floor.)

Inesh Porbudas (10)
Hartley Primary School

The Room Of Wonder

I stood in a room full of fountains
and the water brought light into my life.

I stood in a room full of peace
and the heavens opened amazingly.

I stood in a room full of joy
and the harps played beautifully.

I stood in a room full of dolphins
and their songs sent me into a peaceful sleep.

I stood in a room full of books
and the words played with my mind.

I stood in a room full of fairies
and they danced happily around the world.

I stood in a room full of goddesses
and they hummed a peaceful tune.

I stood in a room full of butterflies
and their colours shone brightly.

I stood in a room full of snow
and the snowflakes bit me till I bled.

I stood in a room full of light bulbs
and they gave me bright ideas.

Henna Ayaz (11)
Hartley Primary School

The Weather Collector
(Based on 'The Sound Collector' by Roger McGough)

A stranger called this morning
Dressed in black and grey
Put every sound in a bag
And carried them away

The swish of the wind
The whistle of the rain
The bang of the thunder
Isn't it such a pain?

The sparkle of the rainbow
The thud of the storm
The crack of the hailstorms
The stillness of the cloud in form

The crunch of the autumn leaves
The plunge of the snow
The sshh of the sand falling
The shining sun which shows

A stranger called this morning
He didn't leave his name
Left us alone silent
Life will never be the same.

Shahida Soomro (11)
Hartley Primary School

Excuses, Excuses

Late again Mirza, what's the excuse this time?
It's not my fault Miss.
Whose fault is it then?
The cat's Miss.
The cat's, what did she do?
It's he Miss. He died.
What about yesterday? You were absent.
Aliens broke into my house Miss, I could not do anything.
Well, where's your jumper Mirza?
In the cat's mouth Miss.
What's it doing there?
The cat ate it.
I thought he was dead.
He is Miss, he ate it and died.
Well go and line up for PE.
Can't Miss, don't have a kit.
Where is it then?
In the bin.
Why is it there?
My friend's dog pooed on it.
Well get out your homework and give it to me.
Don't have it Miss.
Where is it then?
I don't know.
Why don't you know?
Oh can't think of an excuse right now!
How about I'll do it in detention Miss.

Rabia Mirza (10)
Hartley Primary School

A Sea Of Colours

Orange, red, pink and blue,
The colour of the swimming pool
Flows by as I swim through.

Purple, grey, yellow and green,
The colour of fluffy clouds
Part as the sun is seen.

Lilac, turquoise, violet and brown,
The colour of fallen leaves
Dispersed all over the town.

Indigo, pink, black and yellow,
The colour of bananas
And sticky marshmallows.

Silver, white, bronze and gold,
The colour of glistening jewellery
Is priced before it is sold.

Jasmin Sehmbi (10)
Hartley Primary School

What Am I?

I am white and fluffy like cotton wool,
I am silky and tender like a duvet,
I am bland and insipid like stale air,

I am sheer and translucent like fresh spring water
But I can also be opaque and dense like smoke.

I am high altitude like a helicopter,
I can change shape like clay,
I can glide slowly through the air
Like a paper aeroplane.

The answer is quite plain to see,
What am I?

Jules Mattsson (9)
Orchard Primary School

What Am I?

I'm as technical as a fuse box.
I could find any information quick as a flash.
You can access me day or night.
You can use me day or night, but you need some cash,
You can touch my keys,
My keys are as small as a centimetre.
Your fingers move over me like a flash.

What am I?

Yusuf Mohammed (9)
Orchard Primary School

Riddle Poem

When people sleep in me they toss and turn,
Shadows show through the thin material,
You can get me in any colour of the rainbow.
I get out on stiff ground,
I am a compact home.
If you don't put me up properly I will collapse.

What am I?

Zainab Hirsi (10)
Orchard Primary School

A Riddle Poem

I have black as night fur,
I jump on insects to paralyse them,
My fangs are big and prizing,
I shed my clothes for new ones.
Catch me in a web.

What am I?

Tuncay Cager (10)
Orchard Primary School

A Riddle Poem

I am a winged hunter,
I pack a very powerful sting like a splinter.
I'm very caring like a mum,
I don't have any fur.
I can kill a tarantula quicker than a road runner,
I'm creepy, crawly like a maggot.
I'm a powerful killer like a preying mantis.
I'm one of the most successful hunters.
I'm fast like a race car and buzzy like an engine.

What am I?

Julien Winkel Junior (10)
Orchard Primary School

What Am I?

I can see many gardens and fences.
I can hear people speaking and cars.
I am so rainy.
I can smell fresh air and fresh food.
I can see many buildings.
I can see many rocks.
I can see many shops.
What am I?

Jithin Selvamon Selvaraj (9)
Orchard Primary School

What Am I?

I can pick up food that is heavier than me,
I am pitch-black with invisible spots,
I am a feline, smoothly moving through the long grass,
I live in forests and the hot jungles of the southern world.
My razors are as sharp as a knife.

Who am I?

Jasmine Adekunle (9)
Orchard Primary School

A Riddle Poem

We hunt in groups like a pack of wolves.
We are as swift as a bowling ball moving.
We only like things that have been hurt.
We can eat fruit like a human being, but faster.
Our strike force is as powerful as a gale.
We are ruthless killers like the grim reaper.
We have starred in a movie.
We attack instantly like instant tea.
We eat every piece of flesh
Like an obese person eating chicken.
We have big incisors as sharp as a razor.

What are we?

Berkeley Ayemere (10)
Orchard Primary School

What Am I?

I could be tall, I could be small.
Light or dark like the shades of night.
I jump and shout all over the floor.
My clothes are loud just like a bang.
I'm cool and sharp like sheets of glass.
I'm funky and groovy like a 70s movie.
My words are quick they can't be slow.
My chains are called *bling, bling* you know.
On my own or in a group.
I'm the top of the ladder, I'm number one.

What am I?

Romario (9)
Orchard Primary School

What Am I?

I live in holes that I have dug in the ground,
My fur is silky like wool,
I am floppy like a dog,
My tail is white like a cloud,
I am still like a turtle,
I have long ears,
I spring like a kangaroo,
I jump like a frog,
I love carrots as much as lettuce.

What am I?

Yeter Altun (10)
Orchard Primary School

What Am I?

I'm there to stop fights if people are loud.
I risk my life to save theirs, my deeds are heroic.
My uniform is dark but I'm bright inside.
Countries are at war but I cannot help it.
My car is shiny and flies in the night.
The switch of my car sounds like a baby crying,
It goes on forever, but fighting must not.

What am I?

Asma Barits (9)
Orchard Primary School

Magnificent Macaroni

I like macaroni, zacaroni,
tacaroni, cacaroni, acaroni,
yacaroni, sacaroni, pacaroni,
chacaroni, bacaroni.
Yum, yum!

Shannon Palmer-Mutlu (8)
Orchard Primary School

My Big Day

My best bright white vest,
with my best pink dress,
with my best red socks
and my bright orange boots,
I am ready to go now
I've just got to put my
bright pink and purple coat on.
Bye-bye everyone I'm going shopping.
Hello I'm back from shopping.
I'd better go to bed now.
I get dressed in my bright blue night-dress
and I'd better get my bright blue, cute
dog slippers on.
With my dark and light dressing gown
I am ready to go to bed
with my nice, hot, tasty, hot chocolate.
Now that my day is over with,
nighty night little friends
have a good sleep tonight.

Sophie Allen (8)
Orchard Primary School

What Am I?

I can dive up to 200mph as quick as light,
I am a meat eater like a cheetah,
I am as cunning as a crocodile,
My talent is brilliant, I can even kill a bird
Twice my size,
I have feathers which are as soft as silk,
I am a bird killer, like a tarantula creeping around,
I have good eyesight, like an eagle.

What am I?

Abubakar Siddique (10)
Orchard Primary School

What Am I?

I am as silent as a crocodile,
Gliding through the water.
My eyes are as dull as alligators' eyes,
I am as poisonous as a scorpion,
I can move like a worm.
My skin is as scaly as a fish
I can change my camouflage
My teeth are as sharp as a knife.

What am I?

Hanane Taibi (10)
Orchard Primary School

What Am I?

I am as skilful as a clever owl.
My food smells like sweetcorn.
I am as calm as a flowing river.
I am always working hard.
Congratulations.
I will never forget you.
As you grow I will always take care of you.

What am I?

Kwaku Amoah Adamah (9)
Orchard Primary School

What Am I?

I make you go as crazy as a monkey,
You can find me anywhere in the world,
I can make your life change forever.
Addicted.
Without me you are a beggar,
I'm not easy, so *work* for me!

What am I?

Elizabeth Akinyemi (10)
Orchard Primary School

What Am I?

I live under water,
I swim very slowly like a baby.
I love to swim.
I have shining scales.
I have lots of friends under water.
I have gills, fins and scaly skin.
You could get me in all sizes or shapes.
I am rough as a carpet.

What am I?

Kaydene Royes (10)
Orchard Primary School

What Am I?

I am the most agile hunter,
A worthy opponent.
My claws are as invisible as the world's gases.
I have a body which matches fluid.
I run past the plains of Africa,
I am a solitary feline.

What am I?

Richard Bryan (10)
Orchard Primary School

What Am I?

I smell as sweet as perfume,
I am as red as blood,
I look kind and friendly,
But my thorns are like needles.
Can I be your valentine?

What am I?

Sevcan Cigerit (10)
Orchard Primary School

What Am I?

I am so attractive
All the time I am flitting
Like a restless Year 1.
So remarkable, can you believe
I can fly?
Beautiful,
Everyone sees me but I'm scared.
As colourful as a rainbow
Arched in the sky.
People try to catch me,
But I fly.
Always as quick as clicking fingers.

What am I?

Farhana Kazi (9)
Orchard Primary School

What Am I?

I am as hot as burning sand
I am as glittery as golden fish
There are lots of circles around me
You can see me but never touch me
I am dazzling like a smile all the time.

Sevily Kalen (10)
Orchard Primary School

What Am I?

I can roar as loud as a crash of thunder,
I am as soft as a baby's face,
I can run as fast as a Ferrari,
I roam all around the place.

What am I?

Miguel Rels Da Silva (9)
Orchard Primary School

My Friends

My friend's name is Joe
He likes to lick his toe.
My friend's name is Bart
He is as stinky as a fart.
My friend's name is Bertan
He is a fan of Jackie Chan.
My friend's name is Rey Mysterio
You can hear him on the radio.
My friend's name is Fred
He loves to eat mouldy bread.
My friend's name is Samantha
She really wants a panther.
My friend's name is Ray
He is as bright as the day.
My friend's name is Rose
She never picks her nose.
My friend's name is Sam
He fell in love with Pam.
My friend's name is Joy
She acts like a boy.
My friends would like to know you
So we can all stick together like glue.

Ferdos Daqiq (8)
Orchard Primary School

What Am I?

I am an animal
like a large rat
With a big, flat tail.
That lives in and beside a river and lakes.
Felling trees.
Gnawing them to make a dam for a home.

What am I?

Foyez Uddin (10)
Orchard Primary School

My Best Friend Lucas

I had a best friend named Lucas
We made up a name which was Lucas Pucas,
He was very generous and nice,
He could eat a big plate of rice.

Lucas had a very annoying little sister,
He liked to play the game Twister,
He always tried to be cool,
But never did it at school.

Lucas has a kind mum,
Who does not know her sums,
Lucas has a strong dad,
Like nails he is hard.

Lucas drinks Lucozade at lunch,
Which doesn't agree with him much,
He comes out at night.
To give someone a fright.

Lucas loves to eat sweets,
His favourite book was The Twits,
Till today we call him Lucas Pucas,
That's all about my friend Lucas.

Tiwalade Oladipupo (8)
Orchard Primary School

What Am I?

I am the king of the Amazon,
Do not enter,
I live in the thick forests
As big as South America.
My prey will never survive,
Hanging from my mouth
Like clothes in a wardrobe.

What am I?

Corey Fagan (10)
Orchard Primary School

Limericks

There once was a man called The Rock
Who was very hard to knock
He walked through the wall
Kicked a rather big ball
And bent down and smelt his own sock.

There once was a girl called Deva
Who always was sick with fever
She kicked a fat boy
Snatched his new toy
And gave him a hand for a lever.

There once was a man called Knight
Who had never had a good fight
He like to do maths
He guessed all the facts
And not a single one did he get right.

Lucas Lampetis (8)
Orchard Primary School

Please Teacher

Please teacher! No more homework.
Please teacher! Let's have recess.
Please teacher! I know it's only 9 o'clock but
Please teacher! Can we have a break?
Please teacher! Can we play on the swings?
Please teacher! Can we have some fun?
Please teacher! Let's do art instead!
Please teacher! When is it home time?
Please teacher! It's wet play so
Please teacher! Give us the board games please.
Please teacher! Let's play hangman on the board.
Please teacher! I am going now to the toilet.
Please teacher! It's only the sixth time.
Please teacher! It will be home time so can I read a book?

Temi Jekennu (8)
Orchard Primary School

My Alien Friend

My alien friend doesn't like school,
He runs out and goes to the pool.
My alien friend doesn't like my brother,
When he sleeps he pulls the cover.
My alien friend likes nuts and sweets,
When he has a bath the pipe leaks.
My alien friend doesn't follow the school rules,
    In the playground he calls children fools.
My alien friend likes big balloons,
    He plays with them as he watches cartoons.
My alien friend thought Earth was space,
    He then found out he solved a case.
My alien friend can drive a car,
    But he cannot go very far.
My alien friend doesn't wear shoes,
    When I play football he makes me lose.
My alien friend thinks cats are fake,
    When he sees one he says, 'For goodness sake.'
My alien friend is very cool,
    He always comes with me to school.
My alien friend,
My alien friend,
My alien friend.

Bertan Jafer (8)
Orchard Primary School

Animals

My dog saw a frog
The frog is called Mog.
The dog chased the frog
then the frog called Mog
jumped on the dog
then jumped on a log.
The dog ate the frog.

Ilham Abdi (8)
Orchard Primary School

My Friend

I have a friend who is kind
She is able to read my mind
She's as fast as a cheetah
Has a wicked guitar
And jokes that she is going blind.

My friend's name is Tiwalade
She was born on a fine Saturday
She's as black as the night
Has a terrible bite
And she's coming to see me today.

Muberra Keven (9)
Orchard Primary School

Valentines

Valentines, valentines,
How I love valentines
The roses, heart balloons,
You get and you get to share out
All of your love,
I can't wait for the next valentines to come.

Esther Fagbola (8)
Orchard Primary School

Poem Pets

I had a cat
and it saw a hat
it went to bed
and bounced on a bat
and bounced on the mat
and that was that!

Rima Begum (7)
Orchard Primary School

Problems

Every time I come round your house
There's one or two problems,
Tell me are you going dizzy?
Because I can't come in your house,
Is it because you're ashamed
Of something that I can't see?
Did you hide it for all these years?
Tell me what is it?
OK it's a problem that you can't tell,
But this is the problem
I have a rap
Tell me this is it
It goes . . .
Sorry but I can't tell you.

Caleb Guthrie (8)
Orchard Primary School

Autumn Comes

Autumn comes with brown, golden leaves falling like rain
Rainbow colours upon the ground.
Stamping on it makes a crispy sound.
It's like a stranger behind my back.

Autumn comes with squirrels climbing on people's heads
Autumn comes with people visiting the sea.
They watched dolphins jumping up and down
They are free.
Autumn comes.

Jessica Le (8)
Orchard Primary School

My Best Friend Musca

My best friend is as quiet as a mouse
She lives in a massive red house.
My best friend is fine
She likes to drink wine.

My best friend's as busy as a bee
She wants to be like me.
My best friend likes Pie
And she wouldn't have a tie.

My best friend is bright
She thinks she's always right.
My best friend came to the beach
Where she likes to teach.

My best friend likes mud
She drew a lovely bud.
My best friend flew
But she never knew.

My best friend made chicken and peas
Which came out tasting like an ugly tea.
My best friend grew
Some flowers which came out new.

My best friend saw a bat
She quickly put on her hat.
My best friend doesn't cry
But she likes to try.

My best friend has a hood
She also eats yummy food.

Jamila Akter Alam (8)
Orchard Primary School

Summer Comes

Summer comes
with people sunbathing.
Summer comes
with visitors and friends.
Summer comes
with no more school.
Summer comes
with summer past.
Summer comes
with lots of kids buying so much gum.
Summer comes
with lots of ice cream.
Summer comes
with lots of people swimming.
Summer comes
with a big friend as tall as a tree.
Summer comes
with sunny days as bright as lightning.
Summer comes
with people laughing.
Summer comes
with no more adding up to 100.
Summer comes
with no more school rules.
Summer comes
with a summer birthday.
Summer comes
with lots of people.

Nazeerah Mangera (8)
Orchard Primary School

The Fat Cat

That Mike Bad
he is mad.
He's always sad
sometimes glad.
He is cool
he is a fool.
He is always fat
sits on a mat.
Plays with his cat
plays with a bat
his cat chases a rat.
He is happy
changes his cat's nappy.
He is brown
he has a crown.

He is tall
she is small.
She plays with a ball
licks the wall.
He reads a book
takes a look.
It's cold
he writes in bold
his cat gets told.

Nurcan Altun (7)
Orchard Primary School

My Cousin Sally

I got a cousin called Sally
Every day she plays down in the valley.
She is 24
She never answers the door
She likes chocolate cake
When she eats strawberries
She begins to shake.
Every day she goes to a disco
And she wears this beautiful dress
In San Francisco.
Every two years
She goes to Thailand
She sends me postcards
And handmade hairbands
She has blue eyes
She has a big nose
And she never lies
She has a dog
And when it eats a bone
It always feels alone
I've got a cousin called Sally
She likes to play and sing
And when it comes to dancing
She does this special thing.

Elisabeth Ekundayo (8)
Orchard Primary School

Grandpa

I miss my grandpa
He was very funny

I miss my grandpa
He always bought me bunnies

I miss my grandpa
He is a very good listener

I miss my grandpa
he told me interesting stories

I miss my grandpa
The songs he sung always made me cry

I miss my grandpa
He says a question and if it is right he gives me it

I miss my grandpa
He plays with me a lot

I miss my grandpa
He never shouted at me

I miss my grandpa
He tells me jokes and I laugh

I miss my grandpa
He bought my toys

I wish you were here.

Savvina Ploutarchou (8)
Orchard Primary School

My Secret Box

I have a lot of secret things,
I keep them hidden well,
Where I keep them I will never tell.

I have a little brother,
Who is as cunning as a fox,
That's why he is looking for my secret box.

I have a sneaky mum
Who is as clever as a cat
She tried to find out my secrets
When we have a chat.

I have a lovely dad
But he is as blind as a bat
He will never be able to find my secrets
Because it is hidden behind my toy cat.

Oh what have I done now,
I will have to put it somewhere new
And hide it from my family and from you.

Sydni Akiz (8)
Orchard Primary School

Flags

Nigeria, Garner, Liverpool too,
Oh, flags are so funny,
I wish I was one too!
Flags are so colourful,
Like me and you!
Oh, if I had one,
I'd be happy too!
A flag will make me smart,
Intelligent and clever too!
So now you know why I want a flag
And want to be one too!

Demi Daniel (7)
Orchard Primary School

Holiday!

Holiday! Holiday! I go on a holiday
With my friend Pete,
We wore sandals, T-shirts and shorts,
Holiday! Holiday! We had a cat called Pat,
She wore a hat,
Holiday! Holiday! On the trip we went
To the forest we looked for nature
Pete liked to cheat and *eat!*
Holiday! Holiday! When it was bed
I wore a dressing gown and a night-dress,
Pete wore PJs and they tore,
Holiday! Holiday! Me and Pete went to do a tap dance,
Then we went to the beach
I was wearing a swimming suit
Pete wore swimming trunks
And a few weeks later we went home.

Shanara Phillips (8)
Orchard Primary School

Rhyming Poem

I went to bed
Wearing red
I said
Am I dead?

I had a friend,
Wearing white,
Who said
'Are you alright?'

You had a fight,
You were not right,
I had a bike as fast
As a light,
I had to ride,
On my bike
Which I really liked.

Ozan Kaya (9)
Orchard Primary School

Winter

When winter comes round,
You know it's here because of its sound,
The trees lay bare from the autumn wind,
And all the Hallowe'en decorations get binned,
We get ready for a new celebration,
Different ones all over the nation.

The wind sweeps in and brings with it no snow,
And our hopes still stay low,
The rain comes down
And we all wear a frown,
Winter takes up most of the year,
So we hardly get any sunshine all year.

During winter I only like two things,
And it's not when my sister sings,
It's when Christmas comes and I get presents,
But don't eat pheasants,
And my birthday is on the 15th of December.

Milton Johnson (9)
Orchard Primary School

Joe

My name is Joe I don't have anywhere to go.
Can you help me please?
I know I will go to the park and play with a giraffe
And have a good laugh.
'What about me?' said the buzzing bumblebee
'I need a friend too.'
'What you?' said Joe,
'I don't think so,
You might sting my knee.'

Shara Oluwole (8)
Orchard Primary School

My Family

My family is so old
Especially my dad,
My dad thinks he is a lad,
He is sixty-four,
And he likes to play football,
He will never score.

My mum is forty-one,
And she is fun,
She might score,
When she keeps my
Dad at home.

My sister is a real smart pants,
She thinks she knows everything,
She thinks she is so clever,
I bet you she will never wear
Leather.

Well I am the best,
And who can test
The best.

Sarah Parker (9)
Orchard Primary School

One, Two, Three, Four

One, two, three, four
Open up the cabbage drawer
And there I saw
An apple core on the seashore
By the door
On the floor
Now I'm poor
Are you sure
I'll ignore.

Alekzander Crook (8)
Orchard Primary School

My Angel

I have an angel,
She loves me,
She comes so far,
From over the sea.
We try to live
In harmony
And every time
She calls me
Her sweet baby.
I have an angel,
And she cares for me,
Every time I'm in trouble,
She's there for me,
I love her
And she loves me,
She's sweet as can be,
When I put my head
On my pillow,
She watches over me,
My angel's my nanna
Who loves me dearly.

Devinya Thomas (8)
Orchard Primary School

The Sky

The sky is blue
And it comes for you
It is true but the people think it is not blue
But the shape is not like a shoe
And when it rains the sky colour goes grey.

Rafi High (8)
Orchard Primary School

Who Am I?

I have short hair with a little bit of red,
Light brown skin, light brown eyes,
I am beautiful
I have a beautiful smile
I sing a lot
Everybody knows me.
I get a lot of money
My initials are -

K for kind
E for elegant
L for lovely
L for love
Y for young.

Vanessa Idehen (7)
Orchard Primary School

The Vikings!

Noses are red,
My feet are blue,
I have lice in my pants
And rats ate the stool,
Our ship is broken,
Life is stroken,
Lightning strikes,
It hits my Nikes,
Guess what I'm thinking,
It's as fast as lightening,
It's very frightening,
We had to float
In a lifeboat.

Yousuf Mahamed (8)
Orchard Primary School

Santa And The Snake

Santa had a cold
He didn't know what to do
Along came the snake
And told him what to do

So of the snake went
To deliver the present
But when he came back
Santa was having a groove

The snake was looking
While Santa was cooking
'Hey you,' said the snake
'How do you do?'

All the presents are delivered
I've done my part
Oh thank you my friend
What a pal you are.

Fatima Jagne (7)
Orchard Primary School

Myself

I am ready for school!
I have a shower,
Then brush my teeth!
I eat my breakfast,
I go to school and learn,
Sometimes I read a book,
Sometimes we have burgers,
After lunch we go out to play!
Sometimes we go singing with Heather!

Patricia Kyei Acheampony (7)
Orchard Primary School

School Bell Rings

School bell rings,
When I am playing things.

School bell rings,
When I see wings.

School bell rings,
When Mum sings.

School bell rings,
When I have honey.

School bell rings,
When I am funny.

School bell rings,
When I am cutting.

School bell rings,
When I am as hot as a pot.

School bell rings,
When I am rough as a cat.

Dervon Anthony (9)
Orchard Primary School

My Clothes

Slippers are to keep your feet warm.
Caps are for wearing on your head.
Skirts are for wearing in summer and spring.
We wear all this stuff to the beach yah hoo!
We bring a mat and a cat to sit on the mat.
You bring some swimming trunks and some sandals
And a swimming costume yah hoo!
We are going to the beach wearing some trainers
And a jackets and shorts yah hoo!
When they get to the beach
They have to have some of their food.

Jordan Eadon (7)
Orchard Primary School

My Monkey

My monkey he's really funky
He's got fur like a little donkey
He's cool and he ain't a fool
You'll think he's dumb when he chews his gum
But really he's a normal chum
If you go next to him
With a cheeky grin
He'll throw you in a dustbin
He's not a dog so don't yell, sit
He's really fit
Don't mess with him
Just cos he's really slim
You don't know what he'll do to you
He'll maybe do a bit of kung fu
I'm his boss the fairest of them all
But he's the one that went to the ball

He's really tough he's really rough
But the thing is he's not that buff
He's really funny like my old friend bunny
He'll make you dizzy like my best friend Lizzie.

He could be good
He could be bad
But really he's a very good lad
He's spoiled
He's wrecked
So you better *respect!*

Sabrine Abdou (9)
Orchard Primary School

Pub

Alright mate?
Are ya comin' to da pub?
You are skin are ya?
I'll buy ya a drink.
Come on mate -
It'll be fun.

Let's go mate.
So, mate, wot happened?
Ya got mugged by two geezas? Wot?
Ya know who they are, ah? Mate?
Well, then let's get 'em back.
Alright then, get your baseball bat.
Oi! You come ere, ya geeza!
You mug me friend, ah?
Oh yes, ya did!
Woz it him mate?
It woz, ah!

Take dat, ya punk!
Gimme da money now!
And a little extra for da trouble!
And don't ever mess wid me
Or I'll kill ya, ya punk!
Watch out, mate!
Mate, you were going to get smacked!

Wassup wid ya, mate?
Come on, let's go to da pub!
So, mate, why did ya let 'em mug ya?
Cos there were two of 'em.
Ya can't let 'em mug ya.

Punch 'em in da face
And they'll leave ya alone.
Anyway, let's get a drink.
Two vodkas, love!
Thanks darling
Mate, do ya wanna come to da party?
C'mon mate, just come
Alright then, ya don't have to come.
Let's just go home anyway.

Yusuf Abas Qulaten (10)
Orchard Primary School

Butterfly

There was a blue butterfly,
Flying across a blue sky.
There was a beautiful butterfly
Wandering across the blue sea.
There was a bright butterfly
Crossing the blue ocean.
There was a bold butterfly
Crying on the huge tree.

Nowshin Begum (7)
Orchard Primary School

Me And My Friend

I got a friend,
Her name is Vanessa
And we want to play *outside!*
I said please, please,
Can we go out?
Please, because we are sweating
We said thank you,
And we played *together!*

Peri Mustafa (7)
Orchard Primary School

Cats And Dogs

Woof! Woof!
Leave the dog alone.

Miaow, miaow,
Give the cat the phone.

Give the dog the big red book,
So he can sit and take a look.

Give the cat the old grey mice,
Otherwise he'll eat my rice.

Did you give the dog the bone?
Cos he's eating my ice cream cone.

Did you give the cat the phone?
Cos he's sounding in a funny tone.

Did you give the cat the mice?
Thank you that's very nice.
And you can leave the dog alone, all alone,
With his juicy bone, and take care of my pets till I get home.

Fatha Rahman (9)
Orchard Primary School

Toy Boy

Toys are soft,
Toys are hard,
Toys are bad,
Toys are sad,
Toys are strong,
Toys are weak,
Toys are colourful,
Toys are *wonderful!*

Ramazan Calli (7)
Orchard Primary School

Happy

My name is Lappy,
I am always jumping around,
Sometimes when I am happy,
I can be up in the air,
Or down on the ground,
I like listening to different sounds,
Also I am always having a smile on my face.

I am always happy because people make me happy,
If you're happy change your nappy,
When I go for shopping, I feel happy,
Also I feel happy when I go to Hackney
And when my mum buys me something, I feel happy.

When I sit with my friends I feel happy
And when I pass my examination, I feel happy.

Mosthood Olastan (10)
Orchard Primary School

My Fish

My fish is called Silly
That is why I call her silly
Because she hit her head to the wall
The wall, when she is sad and angry
She shakes her fish tank to the wall
And she tips the water out
When someone comes to see her
She jumps out the fish tank to bait them
That is why I call her Silly
When she has a baby
She eats the baby fish
That is because I don't feed her.

Shernice Best (9)
Orchard Primary School

A Poem About My Dog

My dog likes a frog
She plays in the crowd
Every day she barks so loud
Everybody says what's up dog.

She jumps so high
She sings so loud
She says please stand up.

She lays around
She's just so fine
She eats all day
She plays around

She cries all day
Every day she crumples up
All day she digs the garden up
All night she lays around
She wakes up in a terrible fright

She runs so fast
It takes her breath
She stops and says
I wonder in the wood.

She says it was dark
In Victoria Park.

Chevantae Brown (9)
Orchard Primary School

Ali D Rap

I wish my name was Ali D,
I could rap like the Slim Shady,
Look at me in my Ferrari,
Do you see Eddy?
He's so steady,
Let's get ready
To meet Freddy,
He's Punjabi,
I'm doing this MC,
Because I'm crazy
And no one's lazy,
Boogie man's scary,
Because he's hairy,
No one's a fairy.

I wish my name was Ali D,
Listen to my MC,
Do you want a cup of tea?
Listen to this rap with the MPs,
I want to steal a Bentley,
But first I have to get the key,
Otherwise I'll have to pay the fee,
You see,
You can see me on TV
Don't forget you can buy my CD,
And probably a DVD,
Even an Ali D TV,
It's bendy,
It's trendy,
My real name is Ishriaq,
I had a fish attack.

Ishtiaq Ahad (10)
Orchard Primary School

Man U Rap

My name is Dan,
I'm a big fan,
Of Man U,
So are you.

They are fine,
Like red wine,
This is no story,
They get all the fame and glory.

They are the best,
Always better than the rest,
Everyone is cool,
Not one plays like a fool.

Man U are going up,
They'll end up with the cup,
They're not going in the bin,
Actually they're going to win.

Ronaldo's come,
Beckham's his chum,
But he has gone to Real Madrid,
Even though he liked Man U since he was a kid.

I like Man U because they don't get a boo,
And my friends like them too,
Can you see who they are?
They got the big star.

They like Finland,
Except when they're England,
They're Man U,
But they're not new.

That's because I'm a fan,
And my name is Dan.

Daniel Hague (9)
Orchard Primary School

About My Dog Billy!

My dog is silly,
Which is why I called him Billy.
He fancies a dog named Lily.
He fancies another dog called Milly.
He digs a lot and loses the plot.
My dog lives in a basket.
He doesn't like going to the vet.
Oh what a silly pet!

My dog runs after logs.
He's got a friend called Bogs.
He barked at a bee.
He has another friend called Lee.

He likes to run around.
He likes to scratch the ground.
He likes to lie on his bed.
He likes to be fed.
He never gets sad,
But he's always bad.

He likes to go to the park.
He likes to go to the park
So he can bark.
Me and my dog get on.
Me and my dog are the same.
Me and my dog are very lame.
He is always happy.

He doesn't wear a nappy.
He has a big pair of green eyes.
Which makes him easier to be seen.
He acts like a bean when he's ready
But he is always steady.
Me and my dog get on so well.
He likes my computer because it is a Dell.

Ebony Samuel (9)
Orchard Primary School

A Dog And A Cat

A dog goes chasing after the cat
I've never in my life
Seen a cat
So fat
Fat, fat, fat, fat
It's ugly
Ugly, ugly, ugly
It's fast
Fast, fast, fast, fast
With a
Miaow, miaow, woof, woof, woof

The cat's so fast
Fast, fast
The dog came last
Last last
With a miaow, miaow, woof, woof, woof
But the cat
Cat, cat, cat
Saw a sandwich
On the floor
With a
Miaow, miaow
Woof, woof, woof
Bumped
Into a door
With a miaow, miaow
Woof, woof
Woof!

Haboon Hussein Farid (9)
Orchard Primary School

Friends

A boy named Darren
Who was surprisingly barren
He had no toys
Like all normal boys
But he did believe in sharing.
His friend Ned
Came to Darren's house
They ate potato chips in Darren's bed,
Darren's mum said 'Sonny,
It's not very funny,
Why don't you eat people instead.'
Ned's friend Matt,
Bought a large cat.

When he went home
The cat chased a mouse
And shook the whole house,
Darren was watching TV
And saw a boy named Jake
He saw a poisonous snake
It bit his head
And now he's dead,
So that was the end of Jake.
Ned went out and saw a
Boy named Foster,
Caught a mermaid while fishing in Gloucester,
For his lasting regret,
She jumped in the net
And he lost her.

Darren met a boy named Ted
Who always wanted to go to bed
Let's go out to play
OK let's go out to bay.

Claire Troung (9)
Orchard Primary School

Untitled

There was a man called Jack,
Who had a big sack,
But when he fell,
He dropped in well
And couldn't get out again.

There was a fish called Lyn,
Who had a big fin,
Who dropped her dog,
And made a frog,
Who jumped over a log.

There was a girl called Lilly,
Who was very, very silly,
And had a brother called Billy,
Who had a cat,
Which killed a bat.

There was a girl called Helen,
Who loved eating melon,
When she brought a lemon,
She cooked a book,
Which made her fat,
And sat on a mat,
With a cat.

There was a boy called Billy,
Who had a girlfriend called Milly,
Which made the weather chilly,
She had a fight,
And ate a bite,
Which changed her height.

There was a girl called Jane,
Who went down the lane,
Who brought a dice,
And cooked some rice,
Who ate mice for a year.

Jade Luong (10)
Orchard Primary School

All About Koyser

I know a boy called Koyser,
He really likes the toy store,
Whenever he's mad,
He think he's bad,
When he's sad,
I've seen his mother,
With his brother.

He thinks he's a gangster,
When he's a hamster,
He thinks he's funny,
When he eats like a bunny,
When people call him Billy,
He thinks he's silly.

When we're paying attention,
He says it's time for fractions,
He says he's a magician,
When he's an electrician.

When he's got possession,
He says we're on a mission,
When he's supposed to do his session,
When we're supposed to look,
He reads a book.

When we're doing a competition,
He says find your station,
When he goes to school,
He thinks he's cool.

Cos he barks,
We call him Mark,
He says go on the mat,
Or I'll eat your cat.

Kemal Kayran (10)
Orchard Primary School

The Rude Family

Her name is Nelly
She eats too much jelly
She went to her home
So she can moan.

She thinks she's cool
And she plays pool
Her family are rude
But then they are from the moon.

She went to school
And played the fool
Her friend is nice
But she stinks of rice.

Her mum went to the shop
To buy some chops
Her dad went to pay
But he started to play.

Fatima Qulaten (9)
Orchard Primary School

When I Was

When I was sick
I had a friend called Nick
That's when I was
Really, really thick.
When I was fat
I went and bought a cat,
And my cat caught a rat,
When I was eight,
I bought bait,
That is what my sister ate,
When I saw a rat,
It sat on the mat
And it went
Rat-ta-tat-tat.

Hasan Ali (9)
Orchard Primary School

The Ring

A man was walking late and alone
When he saw a skeleton on the ground
A lovely ring on its finger he found
He ran home to his wife and gave her the ring
'Oh where did you get it?' he said not a thing.

'It's the loveliest ring in the world,' she said,
As it glowed on her finger they went to bed
At midnight they woke in the dark outside
Give me my ring a chilling voice cried.

'What was that William? What did it say?'
'Don't worry my dear it'll soon go away,'
I'm coming, a skeleton opened the door,
Give me my ring, it was crossing the floor.

'What was that William? What did it say?
'Don't worry my dear, it'll soon go away,'
'I'm reaching you now I'm climbing the bed,'
The wife pulled the sheet over head.

It was taken from her and tossed in the air
I'll drag you out of bed by the hair
'What was that William? What did it say?'
'Throw the ring through the window, *throw it away!*'

She threw it, the skeleton leapt from the still,
Scooped up the ring and clattered down hill,
Fainter . . . and fainter . . . then all was still.

Malik Adeleke (10)
Orchard Primary School

My Cat

My cat is called Bart,
His fur is black,
He stole a jam tart,
So he sleeps in a sack.

Bart has a cart,
He has a girlfriend,
Her name is Mary
But she's on the lend.

He took her to the park,
They had a hot dog
And they heard a dog bark
But the dog was only chasing after a log.

When he got home
He had a cup of tea,
Bart was so alone
So he called his friend Lee.

When Lee came
They went to a party
It was so lame
So he went back home.

Bart went to bed
He laid down
Then he said
I'm going to sleep like a baby.

When he woke up
He had breakfast
He started eating
Then he thought this breakfast was going to last.

But when he finished,
He found out it did not last.

Christopher Laye (9)
Orchard Primary School

My Idol J-Lo

I had a dream that I was my idol J-Lo,
I would be able to make my own beat rap,
It would be named after my clothes called Gap.

Don't be fooled by the rocks that I got,
I'm still, I'm still Jenny from the block,
Use to have a little now I have a lot,
No matter where I go, I know where I came from.

The Bronx
I was also told I was a little girl,
No matter when I done those twirls,
My mum always told me follow your dreams,
But I just followed my teams.

I've always loved my mum as myself,
Now I'm growing I'm becoming an elf,
I wished my mum didn't leave me alone,
Now she's left me to be J-Lo.

I also have action,
Even though I live in a mansion,
That's what J-Lo's all about,
I'm nearly over my mum, I can't even shout.

I had all those fashion trends,
I might not be able to lend,
My cash is for charity,
Not for my mate Larry.

I'm able to give what I got,
Only for responsible needs,
That's why my movies don't rot,
Also my Mercedes has a whole lot of speed.

Victoria Ghann (10)
Orchard Primary School

Dog Poem

I have a dog
Who's named Frog
Who barks and
Always eats tarts.

He is crazy like
Froggy dogs are
Crazy like my baby.

Always sit on a
Map like a cat
Always silly like
My friend Billy.

Why is my dog,
Silly like my
Friend Billy?

My mum won't
Want this dog why?
Because it is silly
Like your friend Billy!

How many times
I'm going to say
This dummy.

You are like Billy
Silly my dog is sad
When it is bad.

Mum I'm silly
Because I've got
A friend called Billy.

My mum was laughing
We took her to the hospital
To check if she was alright.

Serife Ozicer (10)
Orchard Primary School

My Silly Bat

My silly bat,
He once hurt a cat,
I looked around,
With my feet on the ground,
I went back to my room,
Saw him playing with the broom.

The dinner was ready,
I looked at my best Freddy,
He hit me on my head,
Flew away with my bread.

What a silly bat,
Sitting on a rat,
I hold him in my hand,
He's got my elastic band!

I went to bath,
Saw my clothes in half,
I quickly bathed
And then laughed.

I saw my silly bat,
He bit my dad's hat,
I got it back,
Put it in a sack.

I called my silly bat,
He ripped my toy cat,
I had to repeat this again and again,
What a silly bat.

He ate my ice cream,
I opened the door,
And said 'I don't want no more'
This ain't the law.

Burak Pirbudah (10)
Orchard Primary School

My Cousin Angel

She raps and
Even makes traps
And this is what she says.
'My name is Angel I live
In a cradle,
There is an animal,
That looks like a cat,
I think it is a rat,
But it is a bat,
It's really fat,
I live in a tree,
With a bee and a flea.
I'm so free that I go
With my crew and eat stew.
My room is a crib
If I fib with my bib
I'll break a rib.

Naa Oblikai Laryea (9)
Orchard Primary School

The Things That You Had And Then Didn't

There once was a cat
That wore a hat.
There once was a dog
That slept on a log.
There once was a mouse
That lived in a house.
There once was a bear
That ate a pear.
I have a cat without a hat.
I have a dog without a log.
I have a mouse that lived in a big house.
I have a bear that ate too much pear.

Dillan Al Bayati (8)
Orchard Primary School

My Shiny Diamond

My diamond shines
As bright as the stars
Even brighter than
Big red Mars.

My diamond shines
So very bright
Brighter than the
Full moon at night.

My diamond can
Make night go away
And make my day.

My diamond is
So bright, it makes
Such a light at night.

My diamond always
Shines even in the
Darkest, mines.

My diamond shines
So bright you can
Never be afraid
At night.

Tyler Powell (9)
Orchard Primary School

The Countryside

I was in a countryside
In a loo
When a huge cow came
And shouted 'Moo!'

I was in countryside
Being nice
Although I didn't know it
I had lots of lice.

I was in a countryside
Watching outside
When I was too late
The plants had already died.

I was in a countryside
Eating a pea
Which gave me bad luck
And I hurt my knee.

I was in a countryside
Watching a mouse
Eating something
And that was rice.

I was in a countryside,
Watching the sheep,
When a car came
And did two loud beeps.

Shamol Miah (9)
Orchard Primary School

I Went To The Zoo

I went to the zoo
I saw a kangaroo
His name was Jake.

I saw a chimpanzee,
He was climbing up a tree,
I said 'Count to three'
It said 'kiwi'.

I saw a grass snake,
He wiggled like an earthquake,
He was slimy and his name was Jake.

I saw a bear,
He was very rare,
He was stealing bunches of packed lunches.

I saw a lion,
His name was Bryan,
He was fat as a cat,
He was standing on a mat.

I saw a monkey climbing up a tree,
Like a chimpanzee,
He was climbing branches and stealing people's lunches.

I saw a tiger
He was fast as a cheetah,
He was very strong and very long.

I saw a huge elephant he was stamping up and down,
He was like a silly clown,
I would be happy when he drowns.

Jahed Uddin (9)
Orchard Primary School

Cats And Kitten

Cats are furry
Cats are scary
They are clever and wise
They are full of pride.

Cats chase mice
In a certain way
They chase mice
In their house
They prowl
As well as miaow
Sometimes they bite
And give people a fright
Kittens rip curtains.

Kids are concerned
They might get bitten
If kittens go bad
They turn mad
Cats are careful
And responsible.

I am more confused then I can say
But some cats live in an awful way
All kittens are cute
Because of their looks
Cats scratch
And sometimes snatch.

Monisha Alam (9)
Orchard Primary School

The Flowers

Flowers are sweet
Flowers have lots of sweat
When they sweat they have a scent
When they have a scent, they are attractive.

They are always neat
They use their scent.

They always have coloured hair
They grow slowly in the air
They play games in the fair
When they cry, they have sweet drops.

When it rains
They have no pain
They are good mates
And go on a train.

They have names
Not all the same
They have a frame
Always have an aim.

A flower is cute
A flower has a suit
And wears its boots
Which have a hook.

Stephanie Wong (8)
Orchard Primary School

My Pet

I have a pet that's very kind,
We didn't have anyone to find,
His friend is crazy,
My pet's name is Mazy.

All of the cats are in the kitchen,
But they smell chicken,
There was too much sunlight,
And the cat was on the right.

Everyone was drinking tea,
And they saw a fruit called Pea,
I was proud
My cat was loud.

We went to the sea,
And we saw a bumblebee,
Mazy was on the sand,
That's where aeroplanes land.

It was too hot,
And it was a lot,
The sky was red,
It was to go to bed.

Zaki Muhammed Chowdhury (8)
Orchard Primary School

There Was A Boy Called Jack

There was a boy called Jack,
Who had broken his back.
He thought he was cool,
In class people called him Mark,
Because he always would bark.
When he was at home,
He was a bone.
Sometimes people called him Daisy,
Because he was always lazy.
He was always mad,
Because he was bad.
His mum was angry,
Because she turned into a bun.
He saw outside a broom,
That looked like a room.
He saw a goat that acted like a boat.

Qasim Hussain (10)
Orchard Primary School

Haiku Sun

The sun is merry,
The wind comes round the corners,
Snow falls very fast.

Vishali Patel (7)
St Andrew's JMI School, Totteridge Village

Haiku

The sun is like gold
The sun goes down in the night
You cannot touch it.

Georgina Molloy (7)
St Andrew's JMI School, Totteridge Village

Sun Haiku

Sun
The sun is so bright
The sun has a merry face
The sun is so far.

Mayu Noda (7)
St Andrew's JMI School, Totteridge Village

Haiku

Snowflakes are pretty
In winter I like skiing
Snow is like crystals.

Amani Momoniat (7)
St Andrew's JMI School, Totteridge Village

Haiku

The sun lights the sky
The sun is extremely hot
The sun can burn you.

Christian Tye (7)
St Andrew's JMI School, Totteridge Village

Haiku

The snow falls quickly
The snow falls on the green grass
The snow is like dust.

Marcus Burns (7)
St Andrew's JMI School, Totteridge Village

Haiku

I play in the snow
I like to play in the snow
See the snow falling.

Lily Kinsley (8)
St Andrew's JMI School, Totteridge Village

Sun Haiku

The sun lights the sky,
Sun is super-duper hot,
The sun is boiling.

Sean O'Callaghan (7)
St Andrew's JMI School, Totteridge Village

Sun

The sun is quite bright
It is very beautiful
It goes in the dark.

Cameron Daee (8)
St Andrew's JMI School, Totteridge Village

Haiku Rain

Rain is very hot
Rain can make muddy puddles
Rain makes weird noises.

Sydney Grace Weare (7)
St Andrew's JMI School, Totteridge Village

If Only, If Only

A girl stands in front of me,
Holding a suitcase,
I feel all the hope and happiness
Drain out of me,
I look up to her eyes and say
'If only, if only!'

She says 'It will be OK Jessica,
I'll come back soon.'
A tear trickles down my cheek,
You've guessed haven't you?
That's right, my best friend is leaving me now, forever,
If only, if only.

Jessica Vize (10)
St John's Primary School, Whetstone

Summertime - Cinquain

Summer
Blossom's growing,
Sun blazing up above,
Birds tweeting in the blue clear sky,
Sunshine.

Kelly Warner (11)
St John's Primary School, Whetstone

Small Group Of Big Ants

There was a small group of big ants
And they never wore underpants.
They always left a mess,
But they never confessed,
And that was the end of the ants.

Hamish Nash (9)
St John's Primary School, Whetstone

Kensuke's Kingdom

Lovely adventure,
New boat,
Excited face,
Puffy coat.

Chilly sea,
Challenging night,
Howling wind
Gives me a fright.

Lashing waves,
Drowning fast,
Revolting water,
Dog lost.

Morning island,
Body numb,
Boat please come.

Loud noise,
Woken by night!
Something seen,
Little sight.

Andreas Victoros (9)
St John's Primary School, Whetstone

Valentine - Kennings

Care bearer,
Love bringer,
Heart holder,
Love song singer
Kiss wanter
Long waiter
Hug needer
Come back later.

Jenny Watts (10)
St John's Primary School, Whetstone

Seasons - Kennings

Spring
Flower bloomer,
Sleep awakener,
Smell maker,
Water lover.

Summer
Ice melter,
Plant grower,
Holiday maker,
Frost hater.

Autumn
Colour changer,
Wind bringer,
Fruit producer,
Newborn hater.

Winter
Moon freezer,
Tree breaker,
Morning darkener,
White lover.

Samuel Tan (11)
St John's Primary School, Whetstone

Shark - Kennings

Fish eater,
Fast swimmer,
People scarer,
Single hunter,
Sea ruler,
Everyone hater,
Evil smiler.

Luke Vincent-Kynaston (10)
St John's Primary School, Whetstone

Things I'd Do If It Wasn't For Mum

Chop off my hair and dye it red,
Never, ever go to bed.
Get one thousand piercings in my ears,
Watch horror movies till I'm frightened with tears.
Skip school and say I'm ill,
Steal some money from the Waitrose till.
Spend Mum's money on clothes and food,
Change my name to the coolest dude.
Make best friends with the punks in town,
Dress up like a human clown.
Have water fights with my friend next door,
Wrestle with a wild boar.
Say 'shut up' when I feel like it,
Don't care about life one little bit.
Come to my kingdom and bow,
Hope you know what my desire is now.

Ella Berger Sparey (9)
St John's Primary School, Whetstone

Sick Old Man

There once was a man from Wales,
Who liked to eat bundles of snails,
For he said they were tasty,
But don't be too hasty,
That hungry old man from Wales!

That hungry old man from Wales,
The one that liked to eat snails,
He felt rather sick,
Left the restaurant quick,
That sick old man from Wales!

Fiona Donaldson (10)
St John's Primary School, Whetstone

Kensuke's Kingdom

Adventure began,
Smile on face,
Sailed the seas,
Left no trace.

Crashing sea,
Dreadful night,
Freezing air
Gives me frights.

Overboard!
Sinking quick,
Electrifying storms,
Like a flick.

On an island,
Shadows of night,
Noises everywhere,
Out of sight!

Amber Gharebaghi (10)
St John's Primary School, Whetstone

Three Babies From Mars

There were three babies from Mars,
Who like to play their guitars,
One said to the other,
'How are you my brother?'
And those are the babies from Mars.

There were three babies from Mars,
Who liked to play their guitars,
One played the wrong tunes,
Two, played with balloons,
And those are the babies from Mars.

Despina Kefala (11)
St John's Primary School, Whetstone

Kensuke's Kingdom

Adventure began,
Seeing new places,
Very excited,
Happy faces.

Freezing sea,
Mum's sick,
We're gliding
Very quick.

Feeling numb!
Very homesick,
Trying to hum.

Trying to be bold
And brave,
But feeling cold!
Can't even wave!

Hafsah Rashid (9)
St John's Primary School, Whetstone

Friends - Kennings

Joke maker,
Great truster,
Fun carer,
Game player,
Good sharer,
Secret keeper,
Comfort giver,
Party planner,
Game inventor,
Phone ringer,
Sharing forever,
Lying never.

Eleanor Lovick-Norley (10)
St John's Primary School, Whetstone

Kensuke's Kingdom

New adventure,
Boat brought,
Gone fishing,
Fish caught.

Eat beans,
Mum's ill,
Scary night,
Feel a chill.

Overboard!
I'm sinking,
Can't believe it,
Wasn't thinking!

On an island,
Feeling numb,
How could I?
I'm so dumb.

I see something,
It's my food!
I climbed up there
And then I chewed.

Marc Erbil (10)
St John's Primary School, Whetstone

Growing Up

Big, scary people crowding around me,
Massive, giant teachers,
Lots of children,
Small children below,
I'm tall now,
Huge, grand school,
Loads of homework.
Seven more years to go!

Rosie Stephens (11)
St John's Primary School, Whetstone

Kensuke's Kingdom

Adventure starts,
Bought boat,
Jump aboard,
Write note.

Howling wind,
Terrifying night,
Raging sea
Gave me a fright!

Fell overboard,
Can't get up,
Under water,
Save the pup!

Swim in sea,
Island near,
Climb ashore
Full of fear!

New island,
Where am I?
Here a noise.
Gonna die?

James Thicknes (10)
St John's Primary School, Whetstone

Climbing

C limbing is fun.
L adders, ropes, trees and cliffs are what I climb.
I n the jungle
M onkeys swing in the trees.
B ouncing from tree to tree.
I 'm a monkey and you know it too.
N ow it's time for monkeys to eat bananas.
G orillas have come back from their climb.

Hayley Brooks
St John's Primary School, Whetstone

Things I'd Do If It Wasn't For Mum

Sing karaoke till midnight,
Give next door's cat a big fright!
Shout and scream,
Play the tambourine,
Mess up my hair
When I don't really care.
Paint my bedroom purple and blue,
When it snows, build an igloo.
Buy a pet snake,
Eat loads of cake,
Go and get a mobile phone,
Go and buy a massive new home.
Never bother with smelly old school,
Get some clothes that are really cool,
Steal really cool stuff from the Claire's store,
Shout at the person who lives next door.

Laura Moulton (8)
St John's Primary School, Whetstone

What Am I?

Hair blower
Leaf ripper
Tree bender
Whistle maker.

Window banger
Teeth chatterer
Chill creator
Chaos maker.

What am I?
(The wind)

Olivia Brown (11)
St John's Primary School, Whetstone

What Am I? - Kennings

Sun hater,
Tropical flavour,
Chilling maker,
Child lover,
Seaside enjoyer,
Mouth waterer,
Tasteful smeller,
Taste bud tingler,
Cone filler,
Fast melter,
Flake topper,
Yum, yum.

Answer: ice cream

Maisie Bovingdon (11)
St John's Primary School, Whetstone

Spring Into Winter

Spring
Sunlight,
Birds tweet softly,
Dewdrops shine on flowers,
The sun rises in the cook sky,
Warmth.

Winter
Snowing,
Forests sleeping,
The night fox hides in its home,
The moon hides in the chilled breeze,
Misty.

Kate Hampshire (10)
St John's Primary School, Whetstone

Kensuke's Kingdom

Sinking in sea,
Lost in dreams,
Crashing waves,
Breeze, wind screams.

Lonely on an island,
Frightening night,
Electric storms
Give me a fright.

Annoying man
Bossing me around,
Wonder when
I'll be found?

Starving to death,
Nothing to eat,
Nothing to drink,
No fish or meat!

Mosquito bites,
Burning sun,
Can't make a fire,
But that's been done.

Aastha Bhatt (9)
St John's Primary School, Whetstone

Me And The Sea

On a ship today
All good and ready to play.
Now in sea, cold and numb, me.

Hurt, lonely, scared,
Prisoner, cold, dark,
Scrambled, deserted, me.

Jamie Byrne (9)
St John's Primary School, Whetstone

Kensuke's Kingdom

On an adventure,
Boat new,
Smashing day
With you know who!

Stressed time,
Thrashing waves,
Me shattered,
Seeing caves!

Freezing sea,
Feeling numb,
Windy night,
Hurry, come!

Man comes,
Island mine,
Hurry, come,
Gives me a sign!

Go away,
Hope to find
Peggy Sue,
Quickly come,
Rescue me!

Shiraz Kootar (10)
St John's Primary School, Whetstone

My Mad Hamster

My mad hamster sleeps all day,
My mad hamster likes his hay.
My mad hamster looks around,
My mad hamster smells the ground.
And if you don't think he is mad,
Then I will say you're mad!

Amy Waters (9)
St John's Primary School, Whetstone

Kensuke's Kingdom

New place,
Adventurous boat,
Going round,
Writing notes.

Chilling sea,
Thrashing nights,
Exciting days,
Lots of sights.

Raging waves!
Going now,
Electrifying lightning,
Coming back, don't know how.

Island deserted,
Lonely, scared,
Frightened, annoyed,
If Mum knew, she would have cared.

Noise everywhere,
Can't go back,
Someone watching,
Boiling sun, made a hat.

Catherine Wright (9)
St John's Primary School, Whetstone

Things I'd Do If It Wasn't For Mum

Watch TV and do what I like,
Then go out on my bike.
Go to my friend's and stay up late,
Then go out on a date.
Have some chocolate and some cake,
Then I'd have a Flake.
Paint my room pink and purple,
Then I'd go to the zoo to see a turtle.

Stephanie Hunter (8)
St John's Primary School, Whetstone

Kensuke's Kingdom

Adventure new,
It has begun.
Mum, Dad,
Oh what fun!

Cold night,
Smashing waves,
Sea is calling,
Must be brave.

Electric storm,
Overboard,
I'm sinking quick,
Cannot see.

I stand awakening,
I'm cold,
Frightening calls,
Must be bold.

Noise heard,
Quiet night,
In the cave,
No light.

David Luckhurst (10)
St John's Primary School, Whetstone

Kensuke's Kingdom

Crying to my death,
I float in the sea,
Petrified, terrified, me!

Crashing waves, scared stiff,
Terrifying, powerful sea,
Prisoner, scared me!

Aron Boughton (8)
St John's Primary School, Whetstone

Kensuke's Kingdom

Adventurous beginnings,
Peggy Sue comes,
Mum says yes!
New life begun.

Storm coming,
Scary to see,
Dreadful sight
Confronting me.

Oh no,
Angry sea,
Dog lost,
Drowning me.

Peggy Sue gone,
Out of sight,
Old man came,
Got a fright.

Old man alone,
He seems alright,
Where's his home?
We'll see tonight.

Michelle Kyriacou (9)
St John's Primary School, Whetstone

There Was An Old Lady

There was an old lady of Kent,
Who fell down on top of her tent,
She broke both her arms
And got sent to the farms,
That clumsy old lady of Kent.

Antonia Pagonis (11)
St John's Primary School, Whetstone

Kensuke's Kingdom

Left the house,
On the road,
Nearly there
With the load.

Seen the boat,
Sitting down,
Going to Spain
Without a sound.

Going to Australia
To see Uncle John,
Not far now
To see what's wrong.

Leaving John,
Going away,
Falls overboard,
Going to bay.

Found an island
With a crazy man.
Tried to get me.
I ran! Ran! Ran!

Rhys Hunt (10)
St John's Primary School, Whetstone

Changes

Sunshine,
Flowers bloom,
Juicy fresh fruits grow,
Tweeting birds in the birdbath.
Springtime.

Cold breeze,
Slowly trees die,
Snowflakes fall from the sky,
The wind blows through the misty air.

Christine Edwards (11)
St John's Primary School, Whetstone

Kensuke's Kingdom

Adventure coming,
Boat bought,
Smiles on our faces
And it's short.

Thunder strike,
Roaring lightning,
Oh no,
It's very frightening!

Off boat,
That's bad,
Oh no,
I've gone mad.

Sinking fast,
Help me,
No one here,
Let me free.

Steven Morris (9)
St John's Primary School, Whetstone

Things I'd Do If It Wasn't For Mum

I could go and get the best cat,
I could buy millions of hats,
I could buy the things I like,
I'd love to steal a bike,
Go to a really cool beach pool,
Put make-up on to make myself cool.
Paint my room in spots,
Make myself have dots.
Wear eyelashes that are fake,
Eat the best cake.
I like being me,
But I wish I was free!

Evangelina Moisi (9)
St John's Primary School, Whetstone

Kensuke's Kingdom

Adventure begins,
Boat bought,
All is happy,
Dad drinks port.

Crashing sea,
Shivery night,
Whooshing air,
Feel the fright.

Into sea,
Slowly drown,
Lightning comes,
Gone all brown.

Light of island,
Horrible, lame,
Scared, alone,
Light a flame.

See a shadow,
Frightening thought,
I feel like
I'm in court.

Ming Moore (9)
St John's Primary School, Whetstone

Kensuke's Kingdom

Powerful crashing ocean vast,
Peaceful all alone,
Weak, petrified *me!*

On the ship, now in the sea!
Shivering, numb me,
On this beach, lonely.

Under the crashing ocean!
Begging like my dog,
Waiting for my *death!*

Natasha Solonos (9)
St John's Primary School, Whetstone

Kensuke's Kingdom

My adventures began,
Lashing sea,
Howling wind,
Cold tea.

On the island,
Petrifying dreams,
Living with mosquitoes.
Where's the ice cream?

Wish I was home,
Melting thoughts,
Need the sea,
Rather be taught.

Starving on an island,
It's me he's feeding,
To keep me alive,
I'm pleading.

I've been stung,
Hurts so much,
Can't think now,
It hurts when it's touched.

Bobbie Burkin (9)
St John's Primary School, Whetstone

The Sea

On a ship, all alone,
Waves crashing fiercely,
Sun boiling, beaming, burning.

Waves crashing fiercely,
Feeling all alone,
Prisoner, shivering me.

Me, desolate on an island!
Crashing, bashing waves.
Sun sizzling me.

Laura Martin (8)
St John's Primary School, Whetstone

Kensuke's Kingdom

Away we go,
Adventurous feeling,
Not sure what,
But it is appealing.

Freezing sea,
Soothing air,
Smelly fish,
I don't care.

I'm overboard,
I'm really scared,
My words are frozen,
But I don't care.

Ernestine Hui (10)
St John's Primary School, Whetstone

Things I Would Do If It Wasn't For Mum

Drink lemonade, eat crisps and a cake,
Go to bed when I like,
Always ride my pink and black bike.
Never, ever go to school,
Always be really cool.
Paint my bedroom silver and white,
Buy a cat which is always right.
Get a mobile phone and chat,
Shoo away my least favourite rat.
Be a Tudor, but never die,
Never hear anyone lie.

Pernia Price (9)
St John's Primary School, Whetstone

Ava

My best friend is stunning,
My best friend is great,
My best friend is fab,
My best friend is my best mate!
My best friend is dazzling,
My best friend is sleek,
My best friend is the best,
My best friend is unique.
My best friend is Ava!

Ilana Yacobi (9)
St John's Primary School, Whetstone

My Best Friend

My best friend is the best in the world,
My best friend is Luke.
My best friend is the best at football,
My best friend is amazing.
My best friend is best at maths,
My best friend is so, so, so, so, so nice.
My best friend is the best, and he sticks up for me!

Thomas Magnitis (8)
St John's Primary School, Whetstone

Shark - Kennings

People killer,
Fast swimmer
Blood sucker,
Ocean diver,
Fish eater,
Seal destroyer,
Leg ripper,
Silent waiter.

Meera Patel (11)
St John's Primary School, Whetstone

Things I'd Do If It Wasn't For My Mum

Stay up late and do what I like,
Ride along the streets on my dad's motorbike.
Go and buy a mobile phone,
Break a glass window with a stone.
Bang the piano, shout and scream,
Paint the house blue and green.
Never ever go to school,
Be the queen and always rule!
Go out with my friend Lily,
Buy a dog called Milly.
Go to concerts and always sing,
Buy myself a diamond ring.
Wow! It really is good without my mum!

Jade Kong (9)
St John's Primary School, Whetstone

The Bad Anthony

He is always playing football,
He is always singing badly,
He is always silly and funny,
He has always got big ears,
He is always a big fan of Lord Of The Rings,
He is always the best at football,
He is always greedy,
He is always handsome,
He is always nice to people,
He is always fierce.

Anthony Stamatiou (8)
St John's Primary School, Whetstone

My Mum Says

Wake up,
Get changed,
Eat your breakfast,
Brush your teeth,
Get your things ready,
Hurry, you're late,
Do your homework,
Turn the telly off,
Don't speak with your mouth full,
It's bath time,
Come on, upstairs,
Go to bed.
No!

Jessica Tarling (9)
St John's Primary School, Whetstone

Based On Kensuke's Kingdom

Crashing waves, scared stiff,
Dark, cold, lonely as can be,
Hurt and homesick me.

On our own in the deep sea!
Looking out . . . nothing.
Hurt, scared, homesick me.

Hurt, lonely, scared me,
Looking for someone.
Death coming slowly to me!

Cameron Wolfe (9)
St John's Primary School, Whetstone

My Best Friend

My best friend is Thomas.
My best friend is really funny,
My best friend has very neat writing,
My best friend is as fast as me,
My best friend is amazing at football,
My best friend scores every goal,
My best friend sticks up for me,
My best friend has skill with a ball,
My best friend is intelligent,
He is the best friend you can get.

Luke Erbil (8)
St John's Primary School, Whetstone

Pearl Necklace

The pearl necklace told me,
In a sweet and gentle way,
Please put me on, I'll match your hair,
Oh, put me on I say.
Oh deary me, I don't know what to do,
'Cause what it said seems so very true.
You seem so gaudy, you seem so rare,
But do you think I should take you to a ball
That's over there?
I was tempted to wear it,
I was tempted to see,
And when I put it on, it fitted perfectly,
So pretty, so precious, this is totally me.

Leilah Isaac (11)
Simon Marks' Primary School

The Volcano

The volcano spits out lava,
Gargling dark red seas,
Huffing and puffing at a cigar,
The smoke fills the air.
A bit quieter,
Then a huge roar!
Out gushes lava from his large mouth,
Drowning the sea.
Soon becoming a mass of rocks
To remain for a while.

Beth Oppenheim (10)
Simon Marks' Primary School

Tornado

The tornado sucks
People of the village
Menacingly.
He spun all
Day and night.
He crushes the town
And the village.
The tornado sucks us
Like he's about to
Devour all in sight.

Dean Joseph
Simon Marks' Primary School

In Brighton

I went to Brighton one sunny day,
The big beautiful sun,
I saw it there up in the sky watching everyone.
I also saw the crashing waves on the sand,
It felt like a band!
My heart was pounding like a drum,
And do you know where I was?
In Brighton!
And do you know where that sun was?
In Brighton!

Sarah Brown (8)
Simon Marks' Primary School

Breezing Through The Air

'Breezing through the air,'
Sings the simple teddy bear.

'Breezing through the trees,'
Sing the funny, funny bees.

'Breezing through the sea,'
Sings the fairy.

Ella Davies Oliveck (7)
Simon Marks' Primary School

Winter

Snowflakes are like frozen gems falling
From the grey sky, looking like grey hair on an old woman.
Rain looking like a baby dribbling on the hard, cold ground.
Ice looking like broken bits of glass.
A snowman, the three blocks of ice
Symbolising the past, present and future of winter.

Chantelle Arovo (9)
Simon Marks' Primary School

My Mother

My mother is not one of those women
Who go, 'Oh do I look OK,
Did I put enough make-up on?
Oh I need to lose more weight.'
My mother is short and fit.
She is kind. She rewards me when I'm good.
But the best thing about my mother
Is when we are together
And I can give her a *big* hug and kiss!

Shulamit Morris-Evans (8)
Simon Marks' Primary School

Home Sweet Home

On a farm, the life you lead
Means you have the pigs to feed.
Although they're always smelly,
I always scratch and tickle a belly.

Many people live in the city,
And it's always very busy.
Buses and cars go racing by,
And there are always planes in the sky.

Living by the sea is great,
Except in the summer, that I hate!
Lots of people queue outside
To have a go on the fairground rides!

Jodie Marriott-Baker (10)
Snaresbrook Primary School

Kitten Chaos

Kittens tumble,
Kittens stumble,
Kittens leap
And fall in a heap!

Lying in my bed at night
Their mother jumps on me,
What a fright!

Kittens tumble,
Kittens stumble,
Kittens leap
And fall in a heap!

Playing with balls
Is what they like best,
Except for having a rest!

Kittens tumble,
Kittens stumble,
Kittens leap
And fall in a heap!

Pippa Wiskin (9)
Snaresbrook Primary School

My Ideal Room

My ideal room would
Most definitely be,
Neat, vibrant,
Clean and junk free.

Not too big,
Yet not too small,
With fitted cupboards
And shelves on the wall.

Daniel Morgan-Thomas (10)
Snaresbrook Primary School

My Fears

I'm scared of the dark
And the great killer shark.
I'm scared of big heights
And vampire bites.

I'm scared of killer cats
And big scary rats.
I'm scared of big snakes
And green, swampy lakes.

But most of all I'm scared of someone,
And no, it's not Katie John.
It's a very fierce creature,
It's my headteacher!

Sehar Ishaq Khan (10)
Snaresbrook Primary School

Scared

Scared, scared, scared
Of the dark, and the
Great blue shark with
Piercing eyes like sharpened
Knives and teeth as long as
Blades, with gnashing teeth
He attacks from beneath,
Somewhere near the
Barrier Reef.

Lewis Munro (9)
Snaresbrook Primary School

A Witch!

I saw the black cloak,
Fluttering in the dark,
Blowing in my face,
Flying in the park.

It was flying on a broom,
So thick and so long.
I screamed with a fright,
It was singing a song.

Its face was green,
It fell in the ditch.
I looked up and . . .
Oh no! It's a witch!

Sanjida Mahmood (10)
Snaresbrook Primary School

Zombies

It strikes midnight on the clock,
You are in for a terrible shock,
Zombies rise out from their grave,
To go near one you'd be brave.
You can see them from any view,
Their red eyes beam out at you,
Arms up straight ahead,
Oh my goodness, they are dead!
Try to escape from the cemetery,
Will they get you? Wait and see . . .

Sapphire Sherbird (10)
Snaresbrook Primary School

The Sun

The sun sometimes is a good boy,
but unfortunately has no toy,
he gets bullied about his big head,
which makes him just lie on his bed,
sleeping on his big blanket, the sky,
his worst enemy, the Earth passes by.

He never gets a cold 'cos he's never hot,
he never had a cot,
because he never was a baby,
Whooh! Yeah, maybe,
the sun thinks that the planet Pluto is lazy,
but the others think he's just playing crazy.

Patricia Ogunmodede (11)
Stockwell Primary School

Rose

How sweet is the smell of lilies and roses
As I watch from my window as they pose.
I think of the times that passed us by,
When all I could see was a butterfly
And bluebells that shine.
I think of the way the daisies lay
Beneath the dazzling, clear blue sky.
As I watch the daisies lay,
I think how the days go by.
Missing the days gone by, I see why the light
Shines on them from the clear blue sky.

Jezzell Ethan Domas (11)
Stockwell Primary School

The Four Seasons

I like it in the spring,
When there are many blooming flowers,
But I don't like it when it's April showers.

I like it in the summer,
When the sun comes out to shine.
The days are long, the heat is great
And everybody has got time.

I like it in the autumn,
When all the trees are bare,
It reminds me of someone,
Who hasn't any hair.

I like it in the winter,
When the snow begins to fall,
All the children having fun,
Making snowballs.

Emranur Rahman (10)
Stockwell Primary School

God

God is almighty,
God can be our Lord,
But God is our Father,
So be good for all the world.
The world is full of danger
That's why he made rangers.
Rangers are police who help us in the world,
It is very, very hard for God,
For him to be our Lord,
But thank you God for everything,
I think it's time to say.
Dear God help me do my best,
So I do not make a selfish mistake.
So God, that's why you made the Earth.

Patricia Asante (7)
Stockwell Primary School

Things I Like

My favourite colour is blue,
Like the sky way up high, high, high,
Things I like,
Thinks I like.

My favourite planet is Venus
Where all the cool people come from,
Things I like,
Things I like.

My favourite pets are cats,
The coolest animals in the kingdom,
Things I like,
Things I like.

My favourite author is Jacqueline Wilson,
Her books are so exciting,
Things I like,
Things I like.

My favourite book is Tracy Beaker,
Things I like,
Things I like.

Leilah Clarke (10)
Stockwell Primary School

Pictures

Pictures on the wall,
Pictures on the floor,
Pictures everywhere you go.
Lovely pictures,
Ugly pictures,
It doesn't matter how they are.
A picture of a tree,
A picture of anything
That I can see.

Gabriela Costa (8)
Stockwell Primary School

The Sun

The sun is a bright yellow ball,
The sun, perhaps it's a yellow hall,
The sun maybe is a yellow orange,
Or the sun is a bright challenge.

The sun is never slightly bright,
The sun is always light.
The sun is a golden bun,
But never turns into a gun.

The sun has a brother,
The sun has a mother,
At night the moon is up,
At noon the sun is hot.

The sun can do everything,
But it can never burn out.

Aaron Ford (10)
Stockwell Primary School

Silver And Gold

Today I woke up feeling kinda down
But I called on my best friend, he was not to be found,
But I called on Jesus, my life he can mould,
I'd rather have Jesus than silver and gold.

Silver and gold, silver and gold,
I'd rather have Jesus than silver and gold.
No fame or riches untold,
I'd rather have Jesus than silver and gold.

Silver and gold, silver and gold,
Jesus is better than silver and gold.

Silver and gold will never, ever
Be better than Jesus.
Jesus is so better than silver and gold.

Cherrelle Rule (10)
Stockwell Primary School

Mobile Phone

Hi! It's me on my mobile phone,
I thought I'd give you a call
To say I'm at home.
I stayed up at night
And I can see the light,
It's not a very good sight,
But still I've got my mobile phone.
I start to sing with joy,
It's like my little toy.
I wish I had a friend to call.
I play with my ball,
I'm on my phone at the mall.
I'm so happy,
I'm changing my brother's nappy.

Corrine Burrell Matthews (10)
Stockwell Primary School

Lollipop Lady

A lollipop lady is a jolly good lady,
Who helps us across the road.
A lollipop lady is a jolly good lady,
Who helps us across the road.
Look right, look left,
Look right again, look left.
I go to Stockwell Primary, it's a busy road,
We need a lollipop lady,
A jolly good lady,
To help us cross the road.

Nandipa Mukosi (7)
Stockwell Primary School

The Witch's Kitchen

The witch's kitchen, the witch's kitchen,
Full of colours, wonderful colours,
Full of potions, not a lot of lotions.
Red blood, horrible red blood,
What a kitchen, a witch's kitchen it is!
Argh! What kind of cats are those?
Cats with horns,
Cats with clothes,
Cats with fake nails,
Cats with teeth sharper than a lion's.
Argh! What kind of cats are these?
This is information of the witch's kitchen,
Now you know before you go there!
In this kitchen, the horrible smell,
The smell of old vomit,
The smell of dirty laundry,
The smell of Blair's dirty underwear,
What a kitchen a witch's kitchen is!

Adesola Soyombo (9)
Stockwell Primary School

My Soul

My soul is strong, it can't break,
My soul is a big blood cycle.
Pain hurts and pain flows,
Strong feelings can't go away.
Strong beat, small heart,
I say open my heart like a new bird,
I want to achieve in my work,
But I have to depend on my soul.
One day a tree will grow high and strong
In the garden of justice.

Jeremie Kasonga (10)
Stockwell Primary School

Giant

I saw a giant with
Great big feet,
I'm sure he's not the one
I want to meet.
He's tall and heavy
And far from small,
Wears big clothes
And has a long nose.
I hate giants!

Zhané Fritz (8)
Stockwell Primary School

The Sun

The sun shines bright,
It's going to be great tonight.
But right now
I need to enjoy the peaceful sunlight.

I'm enjoying the sunlight,
But I need to re-write
The poem I made
And I need to go to the super arcade.

Timi Soyombo (7)
Stockwell Primary School

May I Say?

May I say I'm fine today?
I pay my honey to make some money,
Then she shouts to me in glee,
'Hi, Lee,' she said to me.
I'm doing literacy with my sister Lucy, you see.
Go to bed and eat some bread,
Drink some wine, you'll be fine, never mine.

Jhannelle (9)
Stockwell Primary School

The Little Tiger

Once there was a tiger, a poor little tiger,
He didn't want to be tamed,
He just wanted to play his games.

One day that tiger, that poor little tiger, got caught
And was taught to jump through hoops
And do loopy loops.

One day that tiger, that poor little tiger
Remembered he didn't want to be tamed,
He just wanted to play his games.

So that little tiger, that poor little tiger,
Escaped!
And he was no longer a poor little tiger,
He was a happy tiger.

In his games he played . . .
Loopy loop and jumped through hoops!

Ellis Thomas (8)
Stockwell Primary School

Music

Music, choose it, beautiful music,
Beautiful music all day long.
All day long I listen to this bad song.
Beautiful, real, real beautiful.
Bad, my mum said the song's mad.

Music is good, I practice writing it
When I could.
I do my schoolwork when I should,
I rap all day, I rap all night,
But my music will always stay alike.
Music, you're the best,
All right.

Trey Foster Gonzales (9)
Stockwell Primary School

As I Slept I Had A Dream

I dreamed that I was in a jungle
And every time I walked past the trees
There was a noisy bundle of bees.
Bristles in the grass, bristles in the trees,
I was getting scared all the time.

But I was brave, I didn't cry,
Moan or groan, I just got going.
I walked, I talked, but I don't know who to,
I shivered, I wailed, but I don't need *you!*

The tall grass is shaking,
The pretty flowers are flaking,
The trees are drooping down,
What's moving all around
With all this mumbling ground?

Jennelle Reece-Gardner (9)
Stockwell Primary School

The Witch's Kitchen

In the witch's kitchen there's
Slugs and bugs in a potion.
The house is wide, but look inside,
There's nothing but bubbly lotion.

The witch's cats have been fed,
They are not dead.
The witch's hair is green,
The poison frog is as small as a bean.

She looks in the woods at night,
Every time she gets a big fright!
The witch's hair is lovely, but every time I look,
It looks like a rotten old pear.

Shallise Chaney (8)
Stockwell Primary School

All About Me

I have fun
I go on a fast run,
I hate dirty floors,
I love opening doors,
I live an adventure,
I go to the seashore,
I want more,
I go to the menders,
I love watching Tracey Beaker,
My favourite teachers are Michelle
And Mrs Soyombo.
I have a great laugh,
I have a clean bath.
My name is -

  F is for favourite,
  A is for adventure,
  B is for boat,
  I is for ice cream that I love
  A is for actress
  N is for never
  A for ambitious.

A friend never to forget,
Money to bet
This is all about me.

Fabiana Martins (10)
Stockwell Primary School

Love

Love is when you care for others,
Love is when you say people are nice,
Love is when you think people are kind,
Love, love, love,
Love is when you care for others.

Aminah Turay (7)
Stockwell Primary School

My Friends

My friends are kind,
my friends are nice,
they make me laugh
they help me with my work, isn't that so kind.

Sometimes they are rude,
sometimes they are bad,
but all I do is put them on the right path.

Sometimes they are good,
sometimes they are excellent,
some things make them cry so I help them in that way.

My friend smiles all day,
she phones all day
she phones all night

I wish, I wish I had more.

I am so lucky I have friends.

Donica Bryan (10)
Stockwell Primary School

Skull

The truth I tell shall never die
The skull is where it shall always lie
If you tell, it will fade away
Do not tell and it will always stay.
This is a secret for me and you
If you keep it, it shall be true.
Today I die and keep you awake but
If you cry I'll be by your side.

George Foli-Archer (11)
Stockwell Primary School

Dream, Drink, Die And All About Me

I dream I am a ghost,
Just sending post,
My friend drinks,
Her favourite colour is pink.
I don't want to die,
I really like hot apple pies.

Dream, drink and die
It is all about me.

I have fun,
I go on a fast run,
I hate sitting on dirty floors,
I like opening front doors,
I like doing stuff,
I h ate dogs that huff and puff,
I like EastEnders,
I hate going to the menders,
I like Tracey Beaker,
I hate people who are creepers.

My favourite teachers are
Michelle and Mrs Soyombo.

Martina Kissi (10)
Stockwell Primary School

The Stars

I come out when the sun has set
When darkness takes over day
My meeting with the moon
Fills me full of rays.

I sparkle like a diamond ring
Just like winter's shiny snow,
One day I'll become king of the sky
When everyone will shout, *Ho, ho, ho.*

Fatima Islam (11)
Stockwell Primary School

God's Games

God has many wonderful games,
He shows them all to us.
He plays them when we're on the train,
And when we're on the bus.

When the sun is shining,
It means that God is glad.
When there is loud thunder,
It says that he is mad.

If outside it is raining,
God is really, really crying.
It can be of happiness,
Or if one of us is dying.

Now that I have told you
All of God's mysteries,
Just remember when you want something,
All you have to say is please.

Marta Santos Faria (11)
Stockwell Primary School

The Swan

She floats swiftly with all her elegance,
And is as proud as an army of a thousand ants.
The top is calm as you can see,
Under the water is rough,
She's being as fast as she can be.
With her webbed feet she tips, tappers, flip, flappers in the mud,
And she's as beautiful as a rosebud.

Charlotte Louise Corben (10)
Whittingham Community Primary School